Martin Dudley was born in Birmingham and educated at King Edward's School. He studied theology at King's College, London, and has a doctorate in theology. Ordained in Wales, he served suburban, rural and new housing estate parishes before becoming Rector of the Priory Church of St Bartholomew the Great, Smithfield, in the City of London, in 1995. A Fellow of the Society of Antiquaries and of the Royal Historical Society, he is also a Common Councilman of the Corporation of London, a Governor of the City of London School for Girls, and a Director of the City of London Academy in Southwark.

Virginia Rounding has worked with Martin Dudley at St Bartholomew the Great in various roles over the last eight years, and latterly as part-time Director of Development. Following the publication of her critically acclaimed *Grandes Horizontales*, she is currently working on a new biography of Catherine the Great. She also writes reviews for the *Guardian*, the *Sunday Telegraph* and the *Church Times*.

Dudley and Rounding's *Churchwardens: A Survival Guide* was published by SPCK in 2003.

The Parish Survival Guide

Martin Dudley
and
Virginia Rounding

First published in Great Britain in 2004 by
Society for Promoting Christian Knowledge
Holy Trinity Church
Marylebone Road
London NW1 4DU

British Library Cataloguing-in-Publication Data
A catalogue record for this book is available from the British Library

ISBN 0–281–05665–X

1 3 5 7 9 10 8 6 4 2

Typeset by
Pioneer Associates, Perthshire
Printed in Malta by
Gutenberg Press Ltd

For John Forristall Caster,
about to embark on
a 'ministry worth all its pains'

Contents

Introduction:
Gift and responsibility

This is a book about parish ministry and how to survive it. 'Survival' means to make it through the storm; make it to the end of the race; not give in to pressure; outlast one's opponents. It is addressed to the parish clergy and it is intended to be a practical handbook. It is based on the premise that by carrying out careful foundational work many of the problems threatening the life of the church, and the working lives of individual clergy, can be prevented. The skills needed to survive can be learned. The first purpose of the book is to help you prevent things going wrong, its second to help you deal with things that do go wrong. Its third purpose is to serve as an emergency manual, telling you what to do when things have gone really and seriously wrong. We hope that you will not need it for the third aspect. More than that, we hope you will do more than survive, that you will surmount. 'Surmount' means to succeed in spite of; rise above the storm; overcome resistance; transcend difficulties.

To be able to speak of a sense of vocation to ministry and mission, drawing upon one's own conviction and the way in which others have confirmed it, is one of the criteria for selection for ministry in the Church of England. Every priest has, or had at some time, a sense of being called. For the clergy, John 15.16 is a key text: 'You did not choose me; I chose you and appointed you to go and bear much fruit.' The context of the call will have varied. For some it was from within a church context, for others it was outside and brought them to the church and the ministry. After the church has ratified that sense of vocation, each candidate for priesthood is shaped by course or college, by teachers and training incumbents, to be enabled to fulfil that calling to ministry and mission. Each person standing before the bishop will have had expectations and desires, ambitions and fears. Each person will have brought with them strengths and weaknesses, strangely aware that God has often taken the weakness rather than the strength as the defining point. Years into ministry, having charge of one or more parishes and perhaps several congregations, the priest might ponder the extent to which he or she has been able to bear much fruit. Some studies suggest that clergy – some clergy at least, perhaps even the majority – are happy and fulfilled in ministry and find that they are doing what they were called to do. Other clergy, according to Yvonne Warren's study *The Cracked Pot*[1] (published in 2002 and based on research undertaken in 1996–2000) experience, at some time, feelings of irrelevance, isolation, despair, guilt and low self-esteem. Many clergy, of all denominations, are, it seems, close to burnout as they struggle to cope with the ever greater demands that seem to be placed on them.

Ministry is a gift. 'Receive the Holy Spirit,' says the bishop in the ordination rite, 'for the office and work of a priest.' The gift is given not as a burden, but as something to be used to enable you to become, in the service of Christ, what you could not otherwise be or become. The care of souls too is a gift, and in instituting a priest to a parish the bishop says, 'Receive the cure of souls, which is both yours and mine.' The gift is received from someone and the 'someone' in the Church of England who shares the gift which he has himself received, precisely in order to share it, is the bishop. Giving and receiving create a relationship of mutuality and there is more to be found in the relation of bishop and priest than we might expect. There can, of course, be a point where theology and reality part company. Bishops and clergy are human realities and not ideal figures, but the preface to the declaration in the 1980 ordinal states quite clearly and unequivocally that a priest is 'called by God to work with the bishop and with his/her fellow-priests'. The relationship to the bishop is not an optional extra and the church provides a structure for it. It too is intended to be a gift, a means of becoming a community, dispersed but united, serving the Gospel.

Although the relationship between bishop and priest is essential to ministry in an episcopally ordered church, in general the direct authority of the bishop is rarely encountered by the parish clergy, other than when instituted or licensed or when the Chancellor grants or refuses a faculty using the bishop's delegated authority. The full scope and limits of episcopal authority have hardly been tested in the modern Church of England and the relation of bishop and clergy often seems to be based not on canonical obedience but on the principle of 'you leave me alone and I'll leave you alone'. Yvonne Warren found that the perception of many clergy was that bishops were distant: even if they did care, they had no real time to be personally involved in the welfare of the clergy. On a day-to-day basis the clergy deal with archdeacons and rural, or area, deans, and have to cope, within their parishes and deaneries, with the demands of the diocese – originating in the diocesan synod, bishop's council and finance committee – rather than the demands of the diocesan bishop. It might anyway be said of the priest by the bishop, as Prince Kutuzov is reported to have said to the Tsar about the Tsarevich (in Tolstoy's *War and Peace*): 'I can neither punish him if he does wrong nor reward him if he does well.' When the Clergy Discipline Measure 2003 comes into effect, however (probably in 2006), it will increase the ability of the bishop to deal with clergy who are in breach of their obligations or of the ecclesiastical law by making it much easier for the bishop or his representative to pursue a complaint against a cleric, and breaches of other types of regulation might well give rise to disciplinary proceedings of the sort common to other professions. As for reward, there is little to be had in this life, save a word of praise, an honorary canonry or prebendal stall, or recommendation for elevation to higher office.

No one can want an increase in the sort of disciplinary proceedings envisaged by the 2003 Measure and the best way to prevent this happening is by self-regulation. This is not a demand that rests on the church alone; all institutions in the twenty-first century are called to exercise the virtues of transparency and openness. Francis Bridger states in the theological reflection that prefaced the draft of the new *Guidelines for the Professional Conduct of the Clergy* (approved by the General Synod in July 2003): 'No longer are people willing to automatically give professionals the benefit of the doubt. They are subject to scrutiny and criticism in a way that was not true a generation ago. This presents a sizeable challenge to the Church; for it is simply not credible that the Church should expect to remain immune from such scrutiny.' This is a new development in the Church's history and calls for new approaches, not least to the

issues involved in managing human resources. Some of the matters
requiring attention are those that call for the drafting and implementation of various policies – on child protection, disability discrimination, health and safety matters, fire risk management and the
like; other matters are more fundamental to ministry and concern
responsibility, capability (ability to do the job) and accountability.
These are not matters that can be ignored. The initial report of
the Review of Clergy Terms of Service Group (chaired by Professor
David McClean) proposes access to Employment Tribunals to claim
unfair dismissal or breach of Section 23 rights (in the Employment
Relations Act 1999), and greater security for those without freehold,
but also recommends the introduction of capability procedures 'to
be invoked, where a post holder is failing to reach minimum standards', the production of a 'realistic and flexible statement of the
rights, duties and responsibilities of the clergy' (expressed in Clergy
Terms of Service Regulations), and obligatory diocesan ministerial
review schemes and continuing ministerial education. In a major
shift of emphasis, the Review Group recommended 'that the Church
must put in place proper mechanisms to encourage good practice
and to foster deeper relationships of trust and partnership, including the provision of professional human resources advice and
appropriate training for bishops and archdeacons'.

   We are living in a difficult time of transition for the church, for
clergy and laity alike: there is more work to be done by fewer
people; more demands made on fewer resources, financial and
other; the church as an institution is devalued in British society,
while unreasonable demands of virtue and human strength are being
laid on its representatives. Additionally, a culture of complaint
threatens to become as endemic in church life as it is in secular
society. It is, indeed, given legitimacy both in the time-honoured
duty of churchwardens to 'make complaint' and, in the new Clergy
Discipline Measure, in making a written complaint the basis for
the initiation of disciplinary proceedings. It has never been easy to
be Church in the world – it was never supposed to be easy – but
new skills are demanded to meet today's challenging situation if
the clergy are not to be deprived of joy in exercising the gift of
ministry: skills in managing one's own time, in using limited
resources, in decision-making and risk management, in dealing
with a frequently hostile media, and skills required to avoid falling

prey to the catch-all charge of misconduct for 'neglect or inefficiency' in the discharge of the duties of bishop, priest or deacon.

Of course, we might hope and pray that the Gospel we proclaim
and the community of love we espouse will hold back the enemies
of joy and prevent disasters occurring, while ensuring that we will
be able to resolve our differences without resorting to disobedience,
anger, complaint, disciplinary measures, litigation and irretrievable
breakdown. But we also know that we are imperfect human beings
and that weakness is built into, is a necessary condition for, our
ministry. The ordinal reminds us that we cannot 'bear the weight
of this ministry in [our] own strength but only by the grace and
power of God'. And if we still harbour any doubt that the church
and its members always have been and, until time becomes eternity,
always will be prey to the kinds of problem we consider in this
book, we need only listen to St Paul as he exhorts the Corinthians:
'I speak to your shame. Is it so, that there is not a wise man among
you? no, not one that shall be able to judge between his brethren?
But brother goeth to law with brother, and that before the unbe-
lievers' (1 Corinthians 6.5–6).

Clergy of all denominations face significant problems on a daily
basis. We must deal with those problems and their causes, but we
must not allow ourselves to be focused on the problems, real or
imaginary, that seem to beset us. Ministry is, we repeat, a gift. It is
received from God and from the church. We will only be able to
deal with the problems and challenges of ministry if we have a
vision for what that ministry is and should be. We can take various
approaches to expressing the vision. One that we find helpful
derives from the four commandments given by Jesus:

1 Proclaim the Gospel and make disciples.
2 Baptize and incorporate into the church.
3 'Do this in memory of me.'
4 'Love one another as I have loved you.'

These four commandments give a shape to church and ministry. We
are to be proclaimers of the good news of Jesus Christ and we are
actively to seek to make disciples. We are to baptize and to work
to incorporate the baptized into the life of the church. We are to
be eucharistically centred, proclaiming the death of the Lord until

he comes, and all that we do is to be characterized by the love that
Jesus had for his disciples.

These commandments are reflected in the Five Marks of Mission
of the Worldwide Anglican Communion:

1 To proclaim the Good News of the Kingdom.
2 To teach, baptize and nurture new believers.
3 To respond to human need by loving service.
4 To seek to transform unjust structures of society.
5 To strive to safeguard the integrity of creation and sustain
   and renew the earth.

The ordinal, after a rather prosaic list of the work the priest is
called to do, reminds the priest that the treasure entrusted to him
or her at ordination is 'Christ's own flock' and admonishes: 'Serve
them with joy, build them up in faith, and do all in your power to
bring them to loving obedience to Christ.' It also charges the priest
to 'pray earnestly for his Holy Spirit', and continues: 'Pray that he
will each day enlarge and enlighten your understanding of the
Scriptures, so that you may grow stronger and more mature in your
ministry, as you fashion your life and the lives of your people on
the word of God.'

It might have gone further, asking that the priest should daily
receive the spiritual gifts of wisdom and understanding, of counsel
and inward strength, of knowledge and true godliness, together
with the fear of the Lord. These spiritual gifts are needed for the
priest to grow in an understanding of him- or herself and of priestly
ministry. Christian and specifically Anglican traditions of confession,
reconciliation and disciplined prayer should lead us continually to
examine ourselves, to see whether we are indeed doing what God
wants us to do.

When we are admitted to the ministry in a specific parish, those
present are invited to pledge their support for the ministry that we
are to undertake. We cannot know if we are being supported, or
what further support is necessary, if we do not have some kind of
examination. And testing is not simply a question of how well the
clergy are performing but how well priest and people together are
fulfilling their common calling. The clergy do not need to fear
greater scrutiny and accountability. Indeed, it should be welcomed,

but only as a common task of the whole people of God. The majority of clergy want to be effective in ministry. The McClean Review Group went further in stating that 'The great majority of clergy are carrying out their ministry to a high standard.' These clergy want to see excellence in the results of ministry and they are willing to contribute to developing that excellence. A commitment to openness and accountability will go a long way towards removing possibilities for conflict, complaint and disciplinary procedures. Parishes and congregations must also see that they are accountable for their part of the covenant involved in ministry, and it is legitimate to ask whether churchwardens, PCC officers and members, readers, lay workers, and all who accept a part in the totality of parish ministry are doing what they have undertaken to do and doing it in a way that builds up the church. It is also legitimate to ask if bishops, archdeacons, rural and area deans, fellow clergy and diocesan staff are doing what they too are committed to doing.

♦ 1 ♦

Time and resources

What do clergy do with their time?

What do clergy do with their time? This is a question asked by Maloney and Hunt in their study *The Psychology of Clergy*[2] (1991) and they were interested to know initially how much time clergy spent on specific roles rather than specific tasks. They looked at a number of previous studies which had identified and linked roles and activities. A test often required to be taken by aspiring ordinands in the American Episcopal Church – the Inventory of Religious Activities and Interests (IRAI) – identifies ten common ministerial leadership roles and some 240 possible activities; these are the roles:

1 Counsellor: bringing comfort to people in need and helping people with problems.
2 Administrator: planning, promoting, and executing various church-related programmes.
3 Teacher: teaching and directing Christian education in a local church setting.
4 Scholar: scholarly reading, study and research, and/or teaching in a college or on a ministry course.
5 Evangelist: various types of evangelistic outreach and contacting people for Christ.
6 Spiritual guide: talking about religious topics and helping people to develop their faith.
7 Preacher: preaching and public speaking, including other types of public appearances.
8 Reformer: seeking social justice and working for community and/or world improvement goals.
9 Priest: liturgy, conducting public worship, and administering the sacraments.

10 Musician: directing a local church music programme. (This is probably more relevant in an American context, and we might substitute: 'Building manager: maintaining the fabric of the church building.')

With a little adaptation, this list will do to identify the main roles of the Anglican parish clergy. The time we spend on each of them will reflect a number of factors. First may be our internalization of the expectations that others have about our use of time. Among those who have shaped our views will be our first incumbent and those who have befriended and advised us in our parishes. Second, for much of the time we are responding directly to the needs of other people or we are preparing to respond to these needs, rather than serving our own needs. This is true even for something like chairing a meeting, having prepared for it. Third, we will often choose activities based on the approval we get from doing them or the disapproval we generate if we don't do them. The whole parish may know whether or not you visited old Mrs Smith in hospital.

Suggestions for time management

The parish priest, like any self-employed person, is faced with the problem (or challenge) of having to organize his or her working life, without firm guidelines laid down by somebody else, without a 'boss' looking over his or her shoulder, often without the benefit of a separate place to go where 'work' can be clearly sectioned off from 'home' or 'leisure' and where decisions must be made about the time to be allotted to each role. For some people this lack of a structure imposed from outside can be a source of joy, giving a sense of empowerment and freedom. For others it can be a daunting burden. For everyone, the lack of clear boundaries can lead to work becoming all-consuming and overwhelming.

In the absence of structures laid down by an outside authority, it is important for the individual to create his or her own. A priest has an immediate advantage over the secular individual here because of the requirement to say the daily office; prayer, with or without others, can be used to mark both the beginning and the end of the working day. The weekly round of public services also provides the shell of a structure: you know you have to be ready for Sunday, sermons written, notice sheets produced, services prepared, whatever else fits into your working week. For those who work in a team, additional structures will be provided by team meetings and by the division of responsibilities decided upon by the team. The use of certain time slots may be governed by other church staff, if you have any; there may be times set aside for working through correspondence with a church secretary or administrator, for instance, or you may run a system whereby you are available at certain set times during the week to callers enquiring about baptisms or getting married. Whatever your particular situation, however, the bulk of decision-making as to how you spend your time will be left up to you.

There is no dearth of books on time management and this does not set out to be another one, but merely to suggest some pointers on how you might devise a system which works for you. It is worth reading a time management book or two; ones which we would particularly recommend are by Mark Forster: *Get Everything Done and Still Have Time to Play*[3] and *How to Make Your Dreams Come True.*[4] Mark is a life-coach and consultant who has worked in fundraising for the Diocese of Chichester, so he knows a thing or two about how churches and church people work. His website is also worth a visit: <http://www.markforster.net/>. Another useful website to visit is that maintained by John Truscott, who describes himself as a 'church consultant and trainer', at <http://www.john-truscott.co.uk>. He lists a number of useful articles, including training notes on his site; in this context we would recommend his Training Note TN7 entitled 'Ideas for how to make time for life'. It includes sections on 'How to look after yourself', 'How to make time for family and friends' and 'How to make time for spiritual growth'.

Within the Christian tradition monastic rules have been a method of time management for communities of Christians. St Benedict wrote, in his Rule for Monasteries, that idleness is the enemy of the soul and so laid down that the monks should be occupied at definite times in the work of the hands, at other times in reading, and at other times in worship, in addition to the time necessary for cleanliness, eating and, of course, sleeping. Precisely how his Rule was interpreted and times allotted depended on the geographical location of the monastery – what was possible in Italy was impracticable in England – and on the season. It can be worth reading monastic rules when trying to work out a 'rule' for oneself, and it is also worth remembering to incorporate the monastic principle of flexibility in living according to one's rule.

It is important not to become a slave of one's own time management method, but to make it your servant. What is appropriate for one day's work may not be appropriate for the next. One's energy levels vary for all sorts of reasons, physical and mental, and it is sensible to take note of this, rather than to try to force oneself to work with the same speed and consistency day after day. A task that seems onerous to contemplate one day may be accomplished with ease the next. Also, more than in many other professions, a priest may be called upon to change his or her schedule at a moment's notice; parishioners do not die, or have life crises, at times which have been previously entered in their priest's diary. This unpredictability is a major reason to try to be as organized as possible in those areas which can be predicted; leaving such things as sermon writing, production of service sheets, preparation for the PCC meeting and ordering of altar requisites to the last minute is not a good idea.

A change of activity can sometimes be very beneficial. You may be trying to work out some knotty problem and the answer which just won't come to you while you sit at your desk may suddenly suggest itself while you're de-waxing a votive candle stand. Physical exercise can be another very useful thing to build into at least some of the days in your week; going for a regular swim, for instance, may not only be good for your heart but may also help to get your thinking going along unexpected tracks. And it helps to keep you in touch with the world outside the church (until everyone from your church starts to join the same gym or health club, and you end up having PCC meetings in the jacuzzi).

When we are besieged by so many demands on our time, both from other people and from the expectations we place on ourselves, it can be difficult to concentrate on the particular task in hand. Mark Forster suggests a technique which can help concentration as well as help you to achieve a remarkable amount in a short time. He suggests that you work at a series of tasks in concentrated short bursts of activity. He proposes that you divide up the kinds of things that you have to do into no more than ten categories (e.g.

sermon writing, diary management, wedding administration, fabric, family matters, etc., etc.) and then make a beginning by working on each category for a period of five minutes only. Use the kitchen timer to keep you on schedule. Then, the next time round, you increase the slot for each category to ten minutes, and so on, gradually increasing the amount of time spent on each category until the items that need to be done in it are completed. It's surprising how much can get done using this method and it is also very instructive to see just how valuable five minutes can be if used with real concentration. Such a method also helps break down resistance to difficult or wearisome activities – after all, anyone can cope with just five minutes of something disagreeable, and once you have started you may even find it's not quite as disagreeable as you thought. You may not feel like writing a sermon, for instance, but at least in five minutes you can look up the readings, open a new document on the computer, or write the heading in your sermon book, and you might even have time to formulate a few ideas and jot them down. And again, you may not feel – you almost certainly will not feel – that you can tackle filling in yet another faculty application, but at least you could read through the form (again) and start to make a pile of supporting documentation. This is a technique that can work really well when you are feeling overwhelmed by everything you have to do, or when you feel that some important but not urgent things never get done at all because of the pressure of things and people and especially the urgent matters that are not really important. At least with the 'bursting' method you can manage to move everything along a bit. It wouldn't be appropriate to use this method every day – sometimes a particular activity just demands to have all the time and all the attention to itself, needing to be worked at without interruption until it is completed – but it can be a good emergency procedure to come back to when you feel that things are beginning to get out of hand, when you just can't decide what ought to be done next, and when you have at least six things that should have been done yesterday.

Most time management methods feature the 'to do' list (though Mark Forster is not a fan of these, preferring the use of checklists for specific projects and events). 'To do' lists can themselves become overwhelming, paralysing one with the sheer amount of work to be fitted in. There are various ways to approach them. One method is to have a master list, spanning a period of several months, from which a smaller daily list is made. Some people find they work better with a weekly than a daily list. There are computer programs (e.g. Microsoft Outlook or Lotus Organizer) which will manage your lists for you, though there are times when pen and paper seem to focus the mind better than anything else.

If you do use a 'to do' list or task list of some sort, it is worth bearing in mind certain principles:

- **Do not compile an impossible list, and thus defeat yourself before you even begin.** It is important to consider the amount of time you have available, and relate it to your list. It is, for instance, no use having on your list for the day something like 'write a novel' or 'build a new narthex'. These might be on a long-term master list; maybe your list for the month might say 'write chapter one' or 'draft a proposal for the new narthex', while your list for today would read 'write six pages of chapter one' or 'make an appointment to see the architect'. Breaking down your tasks into manageable chunks vastly increases your likelihood of success. Also, there is little point writing down 24 tasks, all of which will take an hour or more to complete, at the start of a working day of seven hours.
- **Prioritize your tasks.** If you are like us and are regularly over-optimistic about how much you can achieve in one day, prioritizing is the only way to survive. By establishing at the start of each day which are the most important tasks to accomplish that day – and either beginning with them or scheduling a time for them which you can guarantee you will stick to – you can ensure that even if you run out of time and don't do all you originally planned to do, at least the most important things will have been done.
- **Remember that you are in charge of your list.** Your list is a tool to help you manage your time; it is not a dictator. Be flexible. If circumstances change during the day, adapt your list to reflect the change. Keep in mind what your priorities are, and try to ensure the change does not unnecessarily knock you off course. Don't be so tied to your piece of paper that you fail to notice what is going on around you.

These three principles are the kind of thing you can find in most time management manuals. Two further recommendations may be added when we are considering time management for Christians, or indeed for any people conscious of their spiritual dimension. These extra instructions are:

- **Trust your instincts (or whatever you want to call that 'still, small voice').** Your list may be telling you there are five urgent things to do immediately, but at the back of your mind there's something nagging – maybe it's a phone call you need to make, someone you need to see, a task which isn't on your list but which is suddenly demanding at least to be started. If your instinct tells you you just have to have a chocolate biscuit before starting work, this is unlikely to be the prompting of the Holy Spirit (though one vicar's secretary always insists that he has a chocolate bar immediately before a PCC meeting, knowing that shortage of sugar leads, for him, to shortness of temper). Something that nags is often something you don't desperately want to do, but we have frequently found that the most important things rise to the surface of one's mind even if they haven't yet made it to the top of the written list. The 'mind' knows what is most important, and none more so than the mind regulated by a daily cycle of prayer and that is at least attempting to be open to the mind of God and the promptings of the Holy Spirit. So, if something is insisting that it must be done, then do it. If, however, you repeatedly find that you need to do things which are not on your list, such that you regularly do not start your list until mid-afternoon, then you are either procrastinating or not compiling your list properly.
- **Forgive yourself and allow yourself to be forgiven.** When you get to the end of the day and you haven't done all you set out to do, don't beat yourself up. Be realistic. If you know you have wasted time, resolve not to waste it tomorrow, but remember that you are human and not a machine. A good day is often followed by a not so good day, the rhythm of life seeming to demand these ups and downs. We also need to recognize that our own measurement of our achievements is limited and incomplete. It may be that something we hardly

noticed, something we said or did, or listened to, or were silent
before, some moment of gratitude for grace received, was what
really mattered today, more than any task we set ourselves.

The lack of clear-cut boundaries in parish ministry can be particularly difficult for people who have come into the ministry from a
more conventional employment situation, who are used to having
set hours and an office, and who, more importantly perhaps, are
able to leave the office at the end of the day. Life is slightly easier
for those who have a parish office, as bounds can be more easily
established between church and home life, while for those whose
'office' is also the study, and really just a room in the vicarage,
boundaries can be decidedly tricky. (The Foundationers at St John's
School, Leatherhead – founded to educate the children of the
clergy – recently made a presentation highlighting the disadvan-
tages in being the children of the vicarage: no weekends away, no
Easter or Christmas holidays, knowing too much about members
of the PCC(!), getting to know all sorts of people who ring the door
bell and end up in the kitchen drinking coffee, and an unhealthily
close acquaintance with the funeral directors.) There is a temptation
either to work every hour that God sends, or else to be available
to every domestic distraction that comes one's way. And that's
without taking into account the doorbell, the phone and the email.
As the information on the Diocese of Durham's website
<http://www.durham.anglican.org/information/collegeofcounsel-
lors.htm> about the Diocesan Professional Counselling Service puts
it: 'Some of the challenges facing clergy can be those of working
in unstructured environments, where they are considered available
at all times and where expectations are often very high and unrealistic. There are problems in living "over the shop"; isolation;
and increased demands in an age where resources are limited and
traditional respect for clergy is being undermined. The knock-on
effects can be relationship difficulties, addictions, and feelings of
guilt, stress and depression, and ultimately, "burnout".'

   An answering machine, or the use of the phone company's
answering service, is a necessity. In one parish, when the new vicar's
wife gave birth to their first child, the churchwardens suggested
putting in a second phone line, with an ex-directory number, solely
for personal use. This has two particular advantages: it separates

the personal from the parochial and it makes paying for telephone calls easier – the parish pays for the parish line, the priest for the private line. A mobile telephone is useful but creates its own difficulties. Many clergy who have given their mobile numbers out to parishioners have ended up changing the number and only giving it to selected people, but a mobile does have caller display, voice mail and text-messaging facilities and can be of great use to clergy who spend a lot of time on the road. Discipline is required in dealing with email. It is advisable to check for new messages at intervals throughout the day, rather than let the computer bleep every half-hour to distract you from what you are doing.

Our experience and the results of various time management studies suggest that the following ideas may also assist clergy in gaining better control of their time:

1 Answer the question 'How do I spend my time?' Look at the list of ministerial roles given at the beginning of this chapter; adapt it to suit your own actual and preferred roles and then rank the roles in order of personal value or preference. Log your time for a full week. You can do this by maintaining an hourly activity record. Some hours will be easy to allocate, such as those devoted to sermon-writing; others will be hybrid and need to be split between categories. Add up the hours and put them alongside each role; finally allocate a rank based on time spent on each role. Compare it with your preferred ranking. In addition to the ministerial roles you may need to add two or three other categories: a) time spent on non-church, non-domestic activities may be needed if you are also a governor of a non-parochial school, a local councillor, charity trustee, etc.; (b) private, family or domestic time; and, in order to be completely honest and because it can be an indicator of possible burnout; (c) undisciplined time devoted to irresponsible, immature, immoral or addictive behaviours (e.g. surfing the web, excessive drinking, inappropriate relationships, sleeping off a hangover, etc.).

2 Build in quiet times when you pause to take stock – they assist in organizing time as well as in dealing with stress.

3 Be realistic about the time required to perform a specific task, and build in a margin of error.

4 Plan for emergencies. You cannot know when they will occur, but sooner or later there will be a crisis, an unexpected meeting or some other unplanned activity requiring your time. Keep space in your diary for the emergency meeting; when it doesn't happen, you can do something else.

5 Have 'next priority' tasks ready to do when someone doesn't turn up, cancels or changes an appointment.

6 Make timed appointments for particular types of enquiry or interview. Some clergy are available at given times on given days. Parisian parishes often display opportunities to see the abbé, one day 'with appointment', another day 'without appointment'. Indicate how much time is available for the interview and draw it to a close in the five minutes before the end. Thirty minutes is sufficient for most matters, and the psychotherapist's 50-minute hour for more significant things (50 minutes' interview, ten minutes for notes and preparing to see the next person).

7 Identify time wasters – among these are people who regularly turn up unannounced, the unfinished tasks that you need to return to later because you didn't allow enough time initially and so now need duplicate 'warm up' time, and the personal disorganization, of office and desk, which means you spend a great deal of time looking for things. (Incidentally, if you are untidy and tend to lose vital pieces of paper, such as applications for baptism or banns forms, it can be helpful to have them printed on brightly coloured paper that is used only for them, e.g. red for baptisms, orange for banns. That way they can be easily spotted in a pile of papers.)

8 Build in time for spouse, family and friends. If you cannot always be with people when you want to be, use notes, telephone and text messages to keep in touch.

9 Learn to work efficiently. If you invest in a computer, invest also in learning how to use it effectively to enable you to do more in less time. Give priority to tasks that multiply effectiveness, e.g. being trained yourself and training others to share roles in ministry.

Some form of 'day book' to record thoughts, objectives, phone calls, requests from other people and 'things to remember' can be invaluable – and certainly must be preferred over a proliferation of messages and reminders written on scraps of paper or stick-on notes which you will inevitably lose.

If you feel that you need more help in time and boundary management than you can find in self-help books, there are some church resources available, though what's on offer varies greatly from diocese to diocese. Top of the list for helpfulness here is the Diocese of Chester whose Leadership Development Programme, aimed at clergy in parish ministry at incumbent or similar level, includes a module covering 'Tools for the Job (and having a life); Effective administration; Managing Use of time; Coping with crises; Developing your prayer life; and All Work and No Play?' If you are fortunate enough to be a priest in Chester Diocese, check out the programme at <http://www.chester.anglican.org/ministry/CLDP/>. The Diocese of Lincoln site refers to a Time Management International Workshop, <http://lincoln.anglican.org/ministry/cme/courses.htm>. The Diocese of Truro seems to offer some good opportunities in its training and development programme (see <http://www.truroworkingtogether.org.uk>). Continuing Ministerial Education (CME) does *not* include training in time management or general organization of oneself. An alternative is to seek help from an outside consultant, such as John Truscott (see Resources for survival in the parish, pp. 131–7).

Time off

It is, of course, important to take time off (though when the first piece of information a visitor encounters about the priest on a parish website is his day off, this doesn't strike one as brilliant PR!). Given the limitations, how much time can you or should you take off? Until the Clergy Terms of Service Regulations proposed by the McClean Report are ratified we have to go by diocesan indications – some of which are non-existent. A priest can be non-resident for three months in any year but has to provide cover, using a priest agreed by the bishop. It is unlikely a priest would actually want to do this every year, but it is a reasonable ambition to strive for – taking ninety days away – once every six or seven years, and to plan to use that time well for rest, recreation and renewal. In ordinary years a priest is generally 'entitled' to six Sundays off, four full weeks' holiday, the inside of a week after Easter and Christmas, and a week for retreat.

A priest should take at least one full day off a week and should aim for this to be evening to evening, giving a full day and two evenings off. One of the problems is that of choosing a day. A priest with a working spouse and school-age children is limited to Saturdays (if his or her day off is to coincide with the free time of the rest of the family) and will lose out when there are weddings. If Sunday is a very demanding day, and it often is, then Monday is a necessary day off to allow for recovery. But then deanery chapter or some meeting of the clergy will be called on that day, and the priest feels obliged to go. (Turning up in casual clothes for a meeting of the deanery clergy with the bishop one Monday afternoon, a priest who usually wore a clerical collar was greeted by the rural dean with the words 'I think Fr D is making a statement.' 'Yes,' said the bishop, 'that this is his day off!' and so it was.)

A priest needs a day off, but also doesn't need to work every waking hour on a working day. A day can be helpfully broken into three parts: morning, afternoon and evening. You don't have to work all three parts. If your evening is going to be given up to another meeting, there is no need to feel guilty if you spend the afternoon reading or cutting the grass or visiting your elderly parents.

Not all clergy find a set day off each week suits their working pattern, preferring to store up several days off and take them in the form of an extra holiday. Whatever you find suits you, and your work and domestic situations, ensure you keep to it. You may find it useful to enlist the help of your churchwardens and/or church secretary (if you have one) in ensuring you get the time off to which you are entitled. We have suggested in our book *Church-wardens: A Survival Guide*[5] that churchwardens should ask such questions as 'Is the incumbent taking sufficient time off?', 'Is he or she taking adequate holidays?', 'Are parish expectations of the priest's role reasonable?' and 'Is the priest finding time for prayer and study?' You might like to ensure that your churchwardens have a copy and that they read it!

There can, however, be a tendency among both church and non-church people to imagine that Christians generally, and priests in particular, must always be ready to respond to any expressed need, no matter how trivial or even mischievous, and to do so with never a cross word, never appearing to be tired (a sign of weakness) and always with a loving smile. There can even be a tendency to expect this of yourself. This is likely to mean that you have a constant sense of failure. You are put in, and put yourself in, a constant 'no win' situation: you are out visiting, and people complain that they cannot get you on the phone. You are in your office/study answering the phone and people wonder why you are not out visiting. It is important to remember that even Jesus could become tired – and the disciples became aware of it and tried to protect him. After hours spent in a crowd, teaching, healing, dealing with people's problems, he felt the need, the absolute necessity, to escape and to find a place of solitude for prayer and restoration of body and soul. St Mark relates (Mark 1.35–37) how the disciples, who only later came to appreciate Jesus' need for solitude, came to search him out saying, 'Where have you got to? Everyone's looking for you!' Follow Jesus' example and when you need it, give yourself a break.

A Christian approach to time management

As we approach the management of time and of events as Christians, that is those who affirm of the risen Christ that all time and all the ages belong to him, we have to do more than deal with a set of plans and schedules. It is not enough to build into our programme time for God – meaning time for corporate worship, public and private prayer, spiritual reading and service of others. Time set aside in that way may be a tithe, an offering to God, but it is not a price we pay to enable the rest of time to be ours. All 'our' time is really God's time. It is a gift to us, and we are to use it well and to account for its use. The verse which comes at the end of part three of Bishop Ken's great hymn 'Awake my soul' is a perfect expression of a Christian approach to time management and reminds us whose servants we are:

> Direct, control, suggest this day
>   All I design, or do, or say:
> That all my powers, with all their might
>   In thy sole glory may unite.

♦ 2 ♦

A clergy ethic and the code of conduct

The new Code of Conduct, or Guidelines for the Professional Conduct of the Clergy (GPCC), is a first attempt – we must hope that it will not be the last – to establish a standard by which the behaviour of clergy can be judged. It is really a compendium of good advice ranging from maintaining parochial registers to note-taking and data protection, from child protection to good administration. (It cannot be reproduced in this book for copyright reasons.) It also contains some curiously opaque lines. What, for example, does 'The clergy minister from their own broken humanity, being aware of their own need to receive ministry' actually mean? Or, to take another example, how should we unpack the following sentence? 'Part of the clerical vocation in both preaching and teaching is a prayerful openness to being prophetic and challenging as well as encouraging and illuminating.' And what might it mean in practice that the clergy have 'a particular role and calling as a catalyst of healing and as an agent of reconciliation for those in their charge' or that 'The call of the clergy to be servants to the community should include their prophetic ministry to those in spiritual and moral danger'? It is not very helpful to mix these statements in with straightforward practical advice and without examining the whole question of a clergy ethic.

An ethic, writes Timothy Sedgwick,[6] has three tasks:

1   to express the purposes that we are to honour and pursue;
2   to make judgements about what should be done;
3   to direct us in a way of life so that we will see and do what is good and right.

As the ordained ministry undergoes assessment and revision, so ethical reflection is expected and is taking place. There is a real danger, however, that it will focus, to the exclusion of the true meaning of ministry, on the hazards of ministry, and in particular on boundary questions. Malony and Hunt (in *The Psychology of Clergy*) see two primary areas of hazard – temptations and stresses – and see temptations solely in terms of sexual indiscretion. They do, however, also recognize an underlying problem. They suspect that 'engaging in *dual-role relationships* is what makes ministry so hazardous'.

By dual-role relationships – which perhaps might more accurately be termed 'multi-role relationships' – they mean those relationships in which ministers play several different roles in relation to those whom they serve. With other 'helping professions' the relationship to patients and clients is generally confined to the office, surgery or consulting room, whereas the clergy interact with their congregations and parishioners in a variety of settings. A priest may hear the confession of a person or counsel a person to whom he or she preaches on Sunday, who is a junior church leader or a member of the choir or a server, whose spouse is a church-warden, who offers help in the parish office, who invites the priest to dinner, and to whom the priest offers comfort in times of sickness and sorrow. It is difficult to keep one's position clear in this multiplicity of relationships. When you add to this the view, expressed by Christina Baxter (to Yvonne Warren in *The Cracked Pot*) that many clergy are 'extraordinarily naive about sexuality', then there really are pitfalls awaiting the unwary in parochial ministry.

The production by the General Synod of Guidelines for the Professional Conduct of the Clergy (GPCC) is part of a process of ensuring that there are clear public expectations about clergy conduct, and that clergy and those to whom they minister are able to define pastoral roles and set and maintain clear boundaries. The revision of clergy discipline procedures is intended both to create equality between the beneficed and unbeneficed clergy and to ensure that there is a proper and objective process for dealing with allegations of clergy misconduct. The development of an ethic is a response to an identity crisis, shared with other professionals, that arises from a breakdown of shared expectations. A clergy ethic is more than the laying down of a code; it involves the identification and exploration of issues facing the church and the clergy, in order to build common expectations that indicate what the clergy should (and should not) do and why, in the context of the total mission and ministry of the church.

Clergy ethics, therefore, must cover more than just the obvious areas of hazard. Five main areas needing to be covered can be presently identified:

1 obligations to self and others;
2 conflicts of conscience;
3 just distribution of services;
4 the use (and abuse) of power;
5 issues in pastoral relationships.

Obligations to self and others

The clergy have a multiplicity of obligations – to God and the Church, to the bishop and those in authority, to family (parents, spouse, children, other relatives), to fellow clergy, to the parish in the broadest sense and to the congregation in the more limited sense, to the maintenance of professional skills and knowledge (through continuing ministerial education), and to themselves ('clergy wellness'). These obligations encompass, in a way, the whole field of clergy ethics.

Conflicts of conscience

Issues of conscience arise from the conflict of obligations. Yvonne Warren found that most of the clergy interviewed had a problem with feeling guilty about not doing enough and in consequence needed reassurance and affirmation. The guilt arises from feeling that expectations are being disappointed. If the expectations – your own, the bishop's, those of your family, congregation or parishioners – are unreasonable, then there is no way out of the cycle of guilt. The only way to survive and to surmount this conflict is to work out a hierarchy of roles and obligations, and to seek broad agreement from interested parties (see Chapter 6, Appraisal and review).

There are, however, certain particular areas that generate conflicts of conscience. A most serious one is disagreement with the teaching and discipline of the Church of England; another, equally serious, is disagreement with the stance taken by your diocesan bishop on some significant matter. The issues most likely to generate conflicts of this sort at present are the ordination of women to priesthood and episcopate, the ordination of openly gay men and women, the marriage in church of those who have a spouse still living by a former marriage, and the blessing of covenanted same-sex relationships. A priest is less like some other professionals who can set up on their own in private practice with few responsibilities to a professional body, and more like a professional – a barrister, for example – whose activities depend on being recognized by a professional body and being governed by it. Some conflicts of conscience will give rise to an act of ecclesiastical disobedience and the priest must be willing to accept the consequences of this in terms of the church's judgement and discipline (something perhaps more likely to happen when the Clergy Discipline Measure comes into operation).

Just distribution of services

In launching the second phase of the London Challenge (a programme of targets for the churches of the diocese to fulfil together by the end of 2007), the Bishop of London made it clear that he was prepared to resign in the absence of a clear commitment to the presence of the church in the parts of the diocese that cannot pay their own way. If other more prosperous parishes would not commit themselves to this, then he could not continue as bishop. The parish priest may also feel that he or she is there to serve the whole parish and not just those whose weekly giving pays the stipend and provides housing. 'Why bother with the housing estate?' a PCC member asks, 'they never come to church.' But the priest knows that the need for the Gospel and for Christian ministry is greater on the housing estate than among the Sunday congregation who have already heard the Word and share in ministry. There may also be conflict between different parishes. In a deanery involving town and village parishes, the town clergy complained about the number of clergy the villages had for a small population but the village clergy noticed that the town parishes, understaffed on week-days, were over-staffed on Sundays. The village clergy took services all day, driving from church to church. The town clergy presided at only one morning service in one church. Today, a priest may well be asked by the bishop to take charge of a nearby parish that has fallen vacant. He or she knows that there are already difficulties coping with current commitments; what answer should the bishop receive? When personnel and resources are limited, there needs to be some agreement about how they are to be used and the task of an ethic is to provide a framework that will enable decision making and resolve conflicting obligations.

The use (and abuse) of power

Although clergy are aware that outside the church they may be considered as rather amusing but irrelevant figures, within the church and in certain contexts they are perceived as powerful, whether they think they are or not. This perception of the power of the clergy is present in whatever model for ministry is in operation: whether that of priest at the altar (with power to bring about the eucharistic change), of charismatic leader (with special gifts of the Holy Spirit), of facilitator and enabler of others (with ability to bring out the gifts that others possess) or any combination of these and other models. Clergy will also be seen as powerful in their ability to accept or refuse applications for baptism and marriage, to distribute offices within the church, and to influence various decisions made in the parish.

The Canons of the Church of England do indeed confirm the authority of the incumbent in a number of areas. Clergy who fail to lead, who are afraid of making decisions and who avoid all possibilities of conflict, are misusing power as much as those who insist on their own way, no matter what. The clergy have an authority that must be exercised. If they fail to exercise it, they create a vacuum, and various people and groups will move to fill it. The clergy are there, in part, to ensure the openness of the church for everyone, and to ensure that it is not controlled by an exclusive clique (not even the vicar's clique).

Clergy can also abuse their power when they deprive people of the rights they have and of the knowledge that they do have such rights. The Canons allow any parishioner to bring a child for baptism, for instance, and the clergy are not to refuse baptism, nor must they place obstacles and conditions in the way of baptism such as to frustrate the intention of the Canons. If a parish priest adopts a baptismal policy that effectively prevents the baptism of babies unless the parents have been attending church for a prolonged period or gone to a particular course, and does not tell the parents of the right of appeal to the bishop against this decision, this is an abuse of power.

A clergy ethic, by providing a framework for the use of the legitimate power of the clergy, must do more than merely prohibit its abuse.

Issues in pastoral relationships

This is the area most people think of when they think about professional ethics. The GPCC say 'There is risk in all pastoral care' but the guidance deals with the place of pastoral meetings, furniture, lighting, dress of the minister, etc. rather than with the real risk. Timothy Sedgwick, reflecting on the literature on professional ethics, identifies four moral issues that stand out here, which may be designated in terms of competence, respect for autonomy, conflict of interest, and confidentiality.

- Ministerial relations depend upon the professional **competence** of the clergy. A priest is expected to have a (better than) working knowledge of Scripture, doctrine, the tradition and history of the Church, liturgy, ethics, and the application of Christian principles to contemporary issues. This competence is needed for leadership, for preaching, teaching, and answering questions. A priest is expected to know how to administer the sacraments validly and how to contract a valid marriage; this knowledge belongs to the duty of care owed to parishioners. As the priest is 'to provide opportunities for parishioners to resort to him or her for spiritual counsel and advice', so the priest must be competent to provide this counsel and advice, and, if in doubt about his or her ability to do this, must seek appropriate training or else refer people promptly to someone else. A priest is not expected to be a trained counsellor working under supervision or a psychotherapist, any more than he or she can be expected to have undertaken research in biblical theology, doctrine, or any other subject. The parish priest is a general practitioner.

- **Respect for autonomy** concerns the way in which we use our competence and professionalism in relation to those who are seeking help, direction or guidance from us. People who are in control of almost every aspect of their own lives and destinies will oddly surrender themselves to a professional, and we see this particularly in the way people accept what 'the doctor says' and allow themselves to lose dignity and personality when in hospital. They can do the same to us. Human autonomy means that a person is self-determining and we have a responsibility to respect that, not to impose our solutions, and to help a person make free and informed decisions.

- '**Conflict of interest**' is another way of addressing the matter of boundaries in ministerial relations and the problem of dual- or multi-role relationships. A number of potential conflicts of interest can be identified that might prevent the provision of pastoral care: relational ('My current relationship to you [as a family member, employer, friend, teacher, etc.] precludes me entering into a pastoral relationship as well'); emotional ('I feel so upset myself about what has happened to you that I cannot counsel you'); psychological ('I am experiencing transference or counter-transference, which precludes further interaction without supervision'); sexual ('I am sexually attracted to you'); professional ('You are my doctor [solicitor, accountant, dentist] and I would find it hard for us to be in different roles').

- Questions of **confidentiality** arise constantly in ministry. The commitment to confidentiality is intended to enable and strengthen the pastoral relationship.

Confidentiality is not the same as the so-called 'seal of the confessional' which is protected in law. If a person asks a priest to hear a confession and the priest agrees, then the priest is bound not to reveal the content of that confession, even in an English court of law. Additionally, the penitent should be aware that the content of a confession is not normally open to subsequent discussion with the priest outside of confession. If a person wants to discuss the subject matter of the confession, it will need to be told to the priest again outside the confessional context, when it will be controlled by the principle of confidentiality but not by the seal of the confessional.

Confidentiality is necessary for other pastoral relationships and it is a serious matter to disclose to another without consent what one has received confidentially. It is also inappropriate for someone who has received pastoral guidance to publish it abroad because the priest, bound by confidentiality, cannot respond to errors or inaccuracies. It is also inappropriate to circulate to other people letters that are marked as confidential to the recipient ('personal and confidential').

A priest ministering to a married couple separately must observe the confidential nature of what is heard from each of them and not become a conduit between them.

A child is as much entitled to confidentiality as is an adult.

A priest may not use knowledge gained from a pastoral relationship in ways that would harm or exploit the person.

The GPCC note two other areas where confidentiality must be respected: in the use of illustrative material in sermons (when personal stories, even about the priest's own family, should not be used without agreement) and the use of data contained in pastoral notes and church files (which we will deal with under Data Protection).

Areas of conflict arise when the priest becomes privy to knowledge that could be used to prevent harm being done to or by another person. This is a very difficult area in which each case is likely to be unique and only one general point can be made: if the priest has good reason to believe that some crime has been committed (e.g. child abuse), then he or she is bound to make that belief known to the appropriate authorities. If the knowledge has been gained only during the course of sacramental confession, the priest is in an even more difficult position, which has not been tested in court. He or she can refuse to give absolution, advise the penitent to confess to the appropriate authorities, and suggest – but not insist – that a further pastoral conversation take place outside the context of the confessional. If no progress is made and the priest still feels that the matter must be brought to the attention of the authorities, we can only suggest that he or she refers the matter to the bishop.

We must give some further attention to the question of the relation between pastoral and sexual relationships, as they, more than any other boundary question, receive the most attention, not least from the media. The GPCC state that 'In their personal life [sic] the clergy should set an example of integrity in relationships and faithfulness in marriage.' Sexual relationships outside marriage, both those that involve erotic contact and those that don't (but are based on sexual attraction), are not, it seems, infrequent among clergy. Any form of sexual behaviour, heterosexual or homosexual, deemed inappropriate to a priest could be considered as 'conduct unbecoming the office and work of a clerk in holy orders' (Ecclesiastical Jurisdiction Measure 1963). The primary area of concern, however, is that of pastoral relationships which develop into sexual relationships. Timothy Sedgwick explains why:

> Some relationships are clearly incompatible with a pastoral relationship, such as when a pastoral relationship changes into a sexual relationship. Whether providing spiritual direction or care and support at a time of crisis, pastoral relations are often marked by intimacy, the need for acceptance and affirmation. Clergy are often idealized as wise caregivers, and for this reason women have been especially vulnerable to the sexual advances of male clergy. The relationship, however, was not begun on equal terms but arose in the context of dependency and idealization. The change in relationship from pastoral to sexual is a change in roles; the boundaries of the relationship have been changed. As this violates the expectations and trust of those seeking pastoral care, such actions are called 'boundary violations.' Not only do they harm individuals, they also undermine a broader trust in the clergy as those able to provide pastoral care.[7]

Yvonne Warren notes that 'many clergy marriages have broken down because a priest has been too zealous in the care of the bereaved and has not been aware of the inherent danger of intimacy. It is within such relationships of pain and hurt that, often unawares, the clergy seek to meet their own needs of affirmation in offering inappropriate care and comfort.'[8] Awareness is the key. It would be unrealistic and foolish to imagine you can operate asexually, with all aspects of sexuality removed from any relationship other than that with your spouse. As the Very Reverend Victor Stock once observed to one of us, 'There is sex in every relationship.' Our sexuality is an innate part of our being, it is one of the ways we relate to every other human being, and it carries a lot of creative energy – it is what we do with that energy that matters. If you are aware, for instance, that a young widow – in her grief, loneliness and desire for comfort – is in danger of transferring some of her sexual feelings on to you (she herself being unaware that this is what is going on), this does not necessarily mean you should refuse to give her pastoral support. It does mean that you have to be exceedingly careful, that you must use your awareness of what is going on to guide her away from an inappropriate focus on you, and that you must never use your awareness to exploit her vulnerability by responding sexually yourself. If you find yourself wanting to do this, then you have more of a problem and you should take care not to be alone with her. But if you were to refuse ever to relate pastorally to anyone with whom you experienced a sexual charge then you wouldn't be able to do much pastoral work!

When problems do arise, there are two distinct scenarios. The first, and the more serious in terms of misconduct, is the priest who exploits the vulnerability of a person with whom he or she is in a pastoral relationship in order to gain sexual advantage. This priest knows what he or she is doing and no amount of advice will prevent them doing it. The second is the priest who is strangely unaware of the hazards of pastoral ministry and, seeking personal affirmation (though unaware that this is what is happening), ends up in a sexual relationship. It is to this priest that the advice in the GPCC is addressed.

♦ 3 ♦

Leadership and governance:
Models and approaches

Authority

The legitimate authority which must be exercised by the clergy is received from the bishop of the diocese whose authority, in turn, must be recognized by the clergy. Canon C 1 (3) of the Canons of the Church of England states: 'according to the ancient law and usage of this Church and Realm of England, the inferior clergy who have received authority to minister in any diocese owe canonical obedience in all things lawful and honest to the bishop of the same'.

The ministry of the bishop is set down in the ordinal. He is there described as 'a chief pastor' sharing with other bishops a special responsibility 'to maintain and further the unity of the Church, to uphold its discipline, and to guide its faith'. He is to 'watch over and pray for all those committed to his charge' and he is to guide those who serve with him 'enabling them to fulfil their ministry'. The role and authority of the diocesan bishop is set down more explicitly in the Canons (C 18), in language that betrays its origins in earlier and older versions. The bishop is the 'chief pastor of all that are within his diocese, as well laity as clergy, and their father in God'. It belongs to his office to teach and uphold sound and wholesome doctrine, to banish and drive away all erroneous and strange opinions, to be an example of righteous and godly living, and to set forward and maintain 'quietness, love, and peace among all men'. Though certain places, the royal peculiars, for example, are exempt by law or custom – custom here meant in a very specific legal sense – from the jurisdiction of the bishop, he has within his diocese what is known as *ordinary jurisdiction*. That is to say, his authority and jurisdiction derive from his office as Ordinary and it is neither delegated to him by someone else, as some of the archdeacon's powers are, nor is it extra-ordinary. The exercise of his jurisdiction can be formally committed to another person, a vicar-general, official, or other commissary, in almost all cases; there are some exceptions, when episcopal authority must be exercised personally.

Within his diocese the bishop is the principal minister and he has the right there of:

- celebrating the rites of ordination and confirmation;
- conducting, ordering, controlling and authorizing all services in churches, chapels, churchyards and consecrated burial grounds;
- granting faculties;
- consecrating new churches, churchyards and burial grounds;
- instituting to all vacant benefices, by collation or by the presentation of others;
- admitting by licence to all other vacant ecclesiastical offices;
- holding visitations, at times limited by law or custom;
- being president of the diocesan synod.

Among other responsibilities, the bishop is required to 'correct and punish all such as be unquiet, disobedient or criminous, within his diocese, according to such authority as he has by God's Word and is committed to him by the laws and ordinances of this realm'. The ordinal says that he 'is to be merciful, but with firmness, and to minister discipline, but with mercy'.

As the bishop leads the clergy, so the clergy are to lead the people. There are of course dangers inherent in such a hierarchical structure, not least that of appearing anachronistic in an age where 'flat hierarchies' are favoured in most other walks of life and where authority is an increasingly difficult, even unacceptable, concept. To operate as a responsible, autonomous adult within a hierarchy is not always easy; just as some members of a congregation may slip towards childishness in their attitude towards 'Father', so a parish priest may find he or she is inwardly regarding the bishop as a headmaster and dreading a summons to the headmaster's study. (In the Society of Mary and Martha's report *Affirmation and Accountability* a parish priest is quoted as complaining:

. . . when clergy get into difficulties or make a mess of something it is possible for bishops to be authoritarian and paternalistic, often leaving clergy feeling patronised and indeed infantilised. On the other hand when clergy need somebody actively to support and be strong on their behalf they can be told that is not the bishop's role and that clergy need to grow up and stand on their own two feet.[9])

Nevertheless, candidates for ordination must 'show ability to offer leadership in the Church community and to some extent in the wider community'. This ability includes capability to

(a) offer an example of faith and discipleship;
(b) collaborate effectively with others;
(c) guide and shape the life of the Church community in its mission to the world. (Criteria for Selection for Ministry)

Yvonne Warren's study of the parish clergy[10] – a random sample of 64 clergy, 37 from a northern diocese, 27 from a southern diocese, chosen from 170 who expressed a willingness to do in-depth interviews – reached some uncomfortable conclusions:

- The largest percentage of clergy are introverted and find it extremely difficult to share personal feelings and expose vulnerability: the idea of being weak is abhorrent to them.
- Many clergy find chairing the Parochial Church Council (PCC) very difficult and its members become 'the enemy'.
- A significant number of clergy are unable to deal with those who disagree with them or to meet conflict situations in the parish.

Whatever model the clergy adopt, they will be looked to as the leaders of the Christian communities committed to their charge. Warren found the majority of clergy favoured the role of leader (based on recognized authority, the possession of expertise, and ability in attracting or inspiring others) or enabler (striving to empower people, enabling them to find their gifts and take on leadership roles) rather than being controlling or confrontational. Several of the clergy interviewed, however, admitted to being diffident, expressing a fear of having to lead, of making decisions, and of facing conflict. It is hardly surprising that none of the clergy identified themselves as confrontational, but those who favour the leadership model will need to be confrontational sometimes. Enablers too, finding their basic approach frustrated by one or two powerful people in the congregation, may also need, reluctantly, to confront them and the obstacle they create. If you are diffident in your approach to leadership – an approach marked by avoidance, vacillation, isolation, alienation and depression – then it really is necessary to seek training in assertiveness and to learn the skills needed for leadership and management. It is no less necessary to seek training if you constantly find yourself trying to resolve conflict by shouting at people, or if you are generally perceived as bossy or difficult.

The roles of leader and enabler are not mutually exclusive. What is needed in a parish is *effective ministry*. It does not matter what name it is given, provided it is effective. Effective ministry will draw on a whole range of approaches, models, charisms and skills, and is likely to be adaptable – soft at the edges, hard at the core, as someone once described Anglicanism. The measurement of effectiveness is the degree to which the mission Christ has given to his church is being carried out. Are people hearing the good news? Are they coming to faith in Christ or having that faith renewed and strengthened? Is the Word being proclaimed and the Sacraments celebrated? Is the celebration of Christian faith marked by joy? These are not unrealistic criteria.

Many parish clergy will find that the *actual* criteria being applied are: Is the parish paying its way? Are we managing to keep the building watertight? Do we have proper policies on disabled access and protection of children? Is there an increase in the number of people attending services?

We will necessarily complain about the latter criteria being preferred to the former, but it is no use spending time and energy on the complaint. We have to pay the quota or common fund; we have to maintain the building; we have to have policies in place; we must be concerned about numbers even if we do not see 'bigness' as synonymous with 'fruitfulness'. If we can, we should enable the laity to deal with finance, fabric and policies, and focus on our faithfulness to the ministry entrusted to us.

Churchwardens

As the parish priest's principal collaborators, the churchwardens share in the exercise of leadership. In our book *Churchwardens: A Survival Guide* we quoted the words of W. S. Wigglesworth, registrar of the Diocese of Derby during the 1940s, and they are worth including here too:

> What is the constant duty of the Churchwardens in this connection is to assist the Incumbent in his work in the parish. It is to the Incumbent that the care of souls is committed, and the part played by the Churchwardens and the PCC must of necessity be secondary to the Incumbent's. Churchwardens, however, have this great advantage over the PCC: the Council is a corporation, but they are human beings; they are therefore in a better position to represent the Incumbent to the parishioners and the parishioners to the Incumbent. Let it be their task therefore to see that each understands the other, that there is peace in the parish, that things temporal are so arranged that all may be well with things spiritual.[11]

Specific duties of churchwardens can be summarized thus (and it is worth remembering that these are *not* the specific duties of the incumbent):

1 To keep proper records, including terrier of lands and inventory of articles belonging to the church.
2 To keep a log-book of alterations, additions and repairs.
3 To inspect the fabric and produce an annual fabric report.
4 To deliver the fabric report first to the PCC and then to the Annual Parochial Church Meeting (APCM), including an account of the inspection they have undertaken and of all actions taken or proposed for the protection and maintenance of the building and the implementation of the quinquennial inspection.
5 To provide answers to the archdeacon's Articles of Enquiry, and complete the annual returns required by the diocese.
6 To present any matters they think ought to be brought to the bishop's attention.
7 To recruit, train and manage the sidesmen.

8 In conjunction with the sidesmen, to care for the safety, warmth and well-being of the congregation.

9 In conjunction with the sidesmen, to maintain order and decency in the church and churchyard.

10 To be responsible for the cleanliness and overall appearance of the church and everything used, or worn, in it.

11 In conjunction with the sidesmen, to take, count, and lock away or hand over to the treasurer collections in church.

12 To attend meetings of the PCC and of the PCC standing committee as *ex officio* members.

13 To act as treasurer if the PCC fails to appoint another of its members to this office.

14 To ensure that the PCC meets its financial obligations.

15 To collaborate and co-operate with the incumbent in the carrying out of all the above duties, and in enabling the incumbent to carry out his or her own specific duties.

16 To have a duty of care towards the incumbent.[12]

In addition to their specific functions and in the carrying out of points 15 and 16 as listed above, you should expect your church-wardens to be one of the major sources of support to you in your leadership role. They are the people who should be able to warn you of any rumbling discontent in the congregation before it becomes a problem; you should also be able to discuss ideas, plans and difficult issues with them in complete confidence. Ideally, they should act as sounding boards for you to try out your ideas before you take them officially to the PCC (the PCC standing committee may also be a forum where you can 'fly a kite').

The PCC

The meeting of the PCC is a significant moment in the life of the parish priest. The incumbent has an obligation, enshrined in the Canons, 'to consult with the PCC on matters of general concern and importance to the parish'. The PCC has to meet at least four times a year and there will be certain types of business that have to be dealt with by the council: appointment of officers and standing committee at the first meeting after the APCM, approval of the annual report and accounts at the last meeting before the APCM,

Articles of Enquiry, faculty applications, and any matters on which the PCC's opinion is sought by the bishop, archdeacon, deanery or diocese.

The role of the incumbent as chairman of the PCC is another one that involves a split. The expression 'Parochial Church Council' means the entire council, made up of ex officio, elected and co-opted members, and the incumbent is an ex officio member. The requirement 'to consult with', and the wording of various other rules (e.g. the PCC 'with the concurrence of the minister') suggest two separate entities, the PCC *on the one hand* and the minister *on the other*. It is this apparent separation that can give rise to a certain antagonism between minister and PCC, with the PCC coming to see itself as a sort of scrutiny committee, examining what the minister has done and giving or withholding approval. In fact the rules are clear that there is no separation and that the PCC is a body made up of clergy and laity, of ex officio, elected and co-opted members, and except in rather rare circumstances there cannot be a valid meeting of the PCC without the presence of, or at least the agreement of, its chairman (the parish priest).

Today, when a priest has charge of a number of parishes, he or she may also have a number of PCCs and/or DCCs (District Church Councils). It would almost certainly not be good use of time to go to all of the meetings, for, even if they limit themselves to four a year, that could mean 8, 12, 16 or more meetings. In such circumstances, and with the agreement of the chairman, the lay vice-chairman can and should chair the meeting in the absence of the priest. It is, of course, sensible for the priest to agree the agenda in advance and for the vice-chairman to ensure that no other matters are deliberately discussed in the absence of the priest, but are referred to a meeting at which he or she will be present. Where this arrangement is normal – as in groups of rural parishes – a relationship of trust between chairman and vice-chairman is essential.

Chairing meetings effectively – so that decisions can be made, owned collectively and implemented – but in a non-confrontational manner, so that conflict is not provoked unnecessarily, is an important skill and one which can be learned. John Truscott includes a very interesting paper on his website <http://www.john-truscott.co.uk> entitled 'How to chair meetings – An Orchestral Approach' in which he likens the skills required by a chairman to those exercised by an orchestral conductor. The aim is to have everyone working together, playing their particular part in a way which contributes to the whole, without anyone dominating, or being left out, which would spoil the 'symphony'. A conductor must exercise authority or the symphony would collapse, everyone playing their own tune without any regard for the rest, but this must be an authority which is accepted and respected by the players. A domineering conductor can terrorize the players into performing woodenly, and not being able to give of their best.

There are certain helpful points to consider when chairing a meeting:

- Make sure you have studied the agenda well in advance, that you have identified areas which may give rise to dissension and have decided how to approach them, and have a rough idea of timings – how long each item should take. Know which items you are prepared to run through quickly or postpone if you run out of time.
- Consider the layout of the room and whether it works well. Does a group of potential dissenters always sit together (and mutter unhelpfully), and is there a way you can tactfully avoid this? – perhaps by asking the members of the standing committee to spread themselves out so that groups are broken up.
- Ask your vice-chairman to take the chair when you want to present an item yourself, so that it does not seem as though it is just the chairman talking all the time and so that people feel more able to contribute to the ensuing discussion. This will also help you not to feel personally under attack if there is less than whole-hearted support for your proposal.
- Consider your body language; ensure your posture shows you are in charge of the meeting (when you are in the chair), that you want everyone to make a contribution but that you will not allow anyone to dominate the meeting by talking all the time.
- Make sure you do not talk all the time! One vicar makes a habit of placing his hand over his mouth during discussions of contentious issues to remind himself to be quiet, let others have their say and not leap in with 'Oh, what rubbish!'

- Do not be afraid to draw a discussion to an end when it has gone on long enough.
- Make sure members understand why they are discussing a particular issue, that they are there to make and own decisions, not to sit around chatting.
- At the first full PCC meeting after the APCM, when there are new members on board, it is worthwhile summarizing the purpose and functions of the PCC and making sure they understand your policies on confidentiality (i.e. what can and cannot be discussed outside a PCC meeting) and what is expected of members.

John Truscott says that the key to chairing a meeting is to get to a position where you are confident in your role, firm in your approach and charming in your manner. We could not agree more!

Measures, canons, rules and regulations

Various aspects of church life are governed by regulation of various sorts. Acts of Parliament and subsidiary legislation are one part of the regulatory bundle, covering marriage, employment matters, health and safety, fire regulations, licensing, historic buildings and VAT. Charity law, which already controls church trusts, determines the shape of the annual report and accounts, and disqualifies certain categories of person from membership of church councils, is likely to have a still greater impact on parishes in future years, especially on those with larger incomes. Ecclesiastical law, contained in measures, canons and rules passed by the General Synod and in subsidiary diocesan rules and regulations, governs everything from the administration of the sacraments to the constitution of the PCC. Regulations may not be very interesting but the minister needs to know what the rules are.

The minister presides at the meeting for the election of churchwardens and the APCM and is the chairman of the PCC. There are rules governing the business of each of these bodies and it is essential that the minister be conversant with them. Failure to follow the rules, especially those concerning elections, generates uncertainty about the validity of the decisions that are made. The rules are contained in two publications: the Churchwardens Measure

2001 and the Church Representation Rules 2004. It is essential that the most recent edition of the Church Representation Rules is used as there have been a number of significant changes since the 2001 edition. The main areas with which the minister should be familiar are contained in part II 'Parochial Church Meetings and Councils', part VI 'Appeals and Disqualifications', part VII 'Supplementary and Interpretation' (especially Rule 48 concerned with casual vacancies) and appendix II 'General Provisions relating to Parochial Church Councils'. This appendix, tucked away at the back of the book, is in fact the essential rule book for the PCC. It sets down the regulations governing the officers of the council, the number of meetings, the power to call meetings, notice of meetings, the chairman, quorum and agenda, order of business, emergency meetings, place of meetings, majority vote and casting vote, minutes, adjournment, standing and other committees and validity of proceedings. Some of these rules, such as the power to call a meeting if the chairman refuses to call one and access to past minutes, can be very significant in the disputes which occasionally arise in parish life.

Example 1: Filling a casual vacancy

It may seem simple enough – a member of the PCC writes to the Secretary to give apologies for the next meeting but also says that, given his failure to attend the last three meetings, he feels he should resign, and does so forthwith. It is February and the member was almost at the end of the second year of his three-year term. What should you do? The answer depends on the date of your Annual Parochial Church Meeting. Rule 48 (1) of the Church Representation Rules 2004 provides (a) that casual vacancies should be filled as soon as practicable after the vacancy occurs, and (b) that a casual vacancy 'may be filled' by election by the PCC of a qualified person but (c) says that this shall not happen if the APCM is to take place 'within the next two months following the occurrence of the vacancy'. Hence, if you receive notification of a member's resignation on 16 February and your APCM is on 15 April, the filling of the vacancy should be left until the annual meeting; if your APCM is on 17 April, you may fill the casual vacancy at the next PCC meeting. The provision for a PCC member says 'may be filled' by election by the PCC; for a Deanery Synod member it says 'shall be filled' (though the two-month rule still applies, suggesting that the APCM should elect a Deanery Synod member if the vacancy falls within the period).

What is a simple and not unreasonable provision for filling casual vacancies can, however, become a weapon in the hands of those who want to disrupt the business of the PCC by constantly raising points of order and claiming that proper procedures have not been followed. There may be a crucial vote, even a vote of confidence in one of the officers, that is carried by one vote. Now if that vote was cast by a person who filled a casual vacancy, the question might be asked 'Was the vacancy properly filled?' Paragraph 17 of the General Provisions attached to Rule 15 states that 'no proceedings of the council shall be invalidated by any vacancy in the membership of the council or by any defect in the qualification or election of any member thereof'. The chairman still needs to ensure that vacancies are properly filled.

Example 2: Conflicts of interest

It is not only the Church Representation Rules that govern the discharge of PCC business. The functions and miscellaneous powers of the PCC are set down in the Parochial Church Councils (Powers) Measure 1956 (printed in our *Churchwardens: A Survival Guide*). A PCC is also, for the purposes of the Charities Act 1993, an exempt charity. Certain charities are exempt from registration because they are considered to be adequately supervised by, or accountable to, some other body or authority. An exempt charity is not subject to the jurisdiction of the Charity Commissioners but is subject to the legal rules generally applicable to charities and to the provisions of the 1993 Act. For PCCs, the principal effect of the Act concerns the accounting regulations (a matter also discussed in *Churchwardens: a Survival Guide*). The members of the PCC are, in effect, trustees of an exempt charity and (to quote the Charity Commission's booklet CC23 – *Exempt Charities*) must

- act reasonably and prudently in all matters relating to the charity
- always act in the best interests of the charity.

The general responsibilities of charity trustees are set out in the Commission's publication on this subject (CC3), available from the

Commission. One particular aspect covered there – the answer to the question 'Can trustees be paid for their duties?' – is of relevance to the PCC. The answer given is as follows:

> Generally, no. Trustees are not entitled to receive any payment out of the charity's property other than reasonable and necessary out-of-pocket expenses. Furthermore they cannot directly or indirectly benefit personally from the charity.

So, can people employed by the PCC (an administrator, an organist, a gardener, a builder, etc.) be a member of the PCC? The answer seems to be 'no', even though there is nothing about it in the Church Representation Rules. The need for the proceedings of the PCC to be utterly transparent would seem to rule out the membership of anyone who is employed by the Council in any capacity because it cannot be clear that, having a financial interest, they can act impartially on any matter that has financial implications.

But there are other sorts of vested interest. Let us suppose that a member of the PCC was also a trustee of another charity that used the church building or the church hall. In general there might be no conflict of interest but there may be occasions (setting the rent, deciding which organizations should be allowed to use the hall) when the member must declare an interest. It will be for the chairman to determine whether the person can be heard on the matter, while not being permitted to be party to the discussion or to vote on the matter. The rules that apply elsewhere must be observed in church matters as well.

Some clergy feel uncomfortable with chairing the PCC because they are paid by the Church of England. The clergy are, of course, office-holders who are not employed and the stipend is not set by the parish or parishes that they serve. This effectively removes any conflict of interest. Nevertheless, there will be business at PCC meetings in which the minister has a personal interest (e.g. the level of expenses) and he or she must declare an interest and, as necessary, hand the chair to the vice-chairman, refrain from voting or even leave the meeting for the discussion.

Example 3: The archdeacon chairs a meeting

An incumbent faced the prospect of introducing a proposal to the PCC knowing that it would be divided. She was deeply committed to the scheme that she was putting forward but fairly inexperienced at chairing meetings. She discussed the matter with the archdeacon and he offered to chair the meeting for her. Was he right to do so?

No, he was quite wrong and the meeting was in consequence not a lawful meeting of the PCC. The Church Representation Rules provide a) that the minister of the parish shall be the chairman, and b) that there shall be a lay vice-chairman elected by the council, and further provides c) that in a vacancy or if the chairman is incapacitated 'by absence or illness or any other cause or when the minister invites him to do so' the vice-chairman shall act as chairman. At the request of the minister, the vice-chairman can act as chairman in order to convene a meeting of the council. It makes sense when the minister is putting a proposal to the PCC or presenting a report, that the vice-chairman take the chair, and this is specifically provided for in the rules. As we have noted elsewhere, this also makes sense in rural groups of parishes or multi-parish benefices, when it is not good use of the minister's time to be constantly attending PCC meetings. The 2004 Rules allowed that the chair could also be taken, if the chairman was not present, 'by a clerk in Holy Orders, licensed to or with permission to officiate in the parish duly authorised by the bishop with the clerk's agreement, following a joint application by the minister of the parish and the council'. If neither the minister nor the other clerk in Holy Orders is present, the vice-chairman takes the chair. Should none of them be available to take the chair for any meeting or for a particular item (e.g. because all three had declared a personal interest), the members choose one of their number to chair the meeting or the particular item. The only occasion on which the archdeacon may chair a meeting of a parish's PCC is when an extraordinary meeting is called (see below).

Example 4: Different types of PCC meeting

The council is to hold not less than four meetings each year. Meetings are convened by the chairman and he or she may do so at any time, giving at least ten clear days' notice. The members may requisition a meeting by presenting a notice signed by not less than one-third of the members of the council. If the chairman refuses to call a meeting or neglects to do so within seven days of receiving a requisition, then the members who signed the notice 'may forthwith convene a meeting' (General Provisions, para. 3). The meeting so convened will be an ordinary meeting of the PCC and the normal rules concerning the chairman apply, i.e. the minister chairs the meeting as usual, or the designated clerk, or the vice-chairman, or a member elected by the meeting, in accordance with the rules. The members cannot simply have a meeting without the minister; only if the minister is absent or asks the vice-chairman to take the chair is he or she not the chairman.

An emergency meeting of the PCC may be called by the chairman at just three clear days' notice in writing to members. The quorum for such a meeting must be a 'majority of the then existing members' and business is limited to that specified in the convening notice. Again, the normal rules for chairing apply.

An extraordinary meeting of the PCC (or an extraordinary parochial church meeting) may be convened by the archdeacon on written representation made to him or her by (a) not less than one-third of the lay members of the PCC or (b) by one-tenth of the persons whose names are on the electoral roll of the parish, if such application is deemed by the archdeacon 'to have been made with sufficient cause'. The archdeacon then, and only then, takes the chair or appoints a chairman to preside. The chairman of that extraordinary meeting, unless otherwise entitled to attend the meeting, would have no vote. The minister, being a member of the PCC, could, of course, attend the meeting, speak and vote, but is prohibited from taking the chair.

Functions of the PCC

The specific duties of the PCC can be summarized as follows:

1 To care for, maintain, preserve and take out adequate insurance cover for the fabric, goods and ornaments of the church.
2 To agree a budget and to be responsible for the income and expenditure of the parish.
3 To keep proper financial records and accounting procedures.
4 To prepare annual financial statements and an annual report, and present them to the APCM.
5 To arrange for independent examination or audit of the financial statements.

6   To consult with the incumbent on matters of general concern and importance to the parish.
7   To co-operate with the incumbent in promoting the mission of the Church.[13]

Finally, it is worth listing the specific **duties of the minister** (particularly as there is often confusion among PCC members over what they can legitimately 'interfere' in and what is primarily under your control):

1   To celebrate the Eucharist (or cause it to be celebrated in his or her absence) and administer the other rites and sacraments of the Church.
2   To be responsible for liturgy.
3   To have ultimate responsibility for music performed during the liturgy, in co-operation with the director of music, organist or choirmaster.
4   To preach (or cause to be preached) at least one sermon every Sunday.
5   To instruct parishioners in the Christian faith.
6   To prepare candidates for confirmation.
7   To visit the sick.
8   To be prepared to make himself or herself available to parishioners seeking spiritual counsel and advice.
9   To be diligent in prayer and study.
10 To chair the PCC, the PCC standing committee and the APCM.
11 To consult with the PCC.
12 To co-operate with the churchwardens.[14]

Teambuilding

Part of the work of enabling others to share in leadership involves seeking out, nurturing and developing future PCC members and potential churchwardens. In short, a priest will want to:

* maintain a good working relationship with the churchwardens;
* be certain that he or she enjoys the confidence of the majority of the PCC;

- spend time developing the lay leadership of the parish, including looking for and encouraging possible candidates for election to office.

In seeking to work effectively with churchwardens, PCC members and others it is worth consulting some of the material available on teamworking in industry. Teambuilding Inc. has some interesting material on its website <http://www.teambuildinginc.com>, including an article by Jay K. Cherney on 'Appreciative Teambuilding'. He writes that the appreciative approach to improving human systems has an extraordinary power to unleash enthusiasm and momentum for positive change. Traditional ways of improving teamwork have often begun by assessing what isn't working in order to repair it; by contrast, the appreciative approach starts with a series of questions about what is working, in order to uncover the root causes of team success. The stages of what is termed 'appreciative inquiry' are:

1 discover the best of what is;
2 envision what might be;
3 dialogue over what should be;
4 innovate what will be.

Encouraging a positive frame of mind in your PCC members and church officers and affirming appreciatively what they do does not mean denying negative emotions or refusing to acknowledge sources of conflict or distress. It does mean recognizing that just as 'positive thinking' may help to ease personal stress, so having a positive attitude as a group encourages improvement, the generating of good ideas and implementing them with energy. An important maxim of appreciative inquiry is 'What we focus on expands'. In other words, to focus on what works and do more of it achieves better results than focusing on what doesn't work and trying to do less of it. Too much attention to the causes of conflict can sometimes entangle us and actually deepen dissension. Ensuring that everyone in a team shares the same vision and is focused on bringing it to fruition is an important aspect of leadership.

♦ 4 ♦

Protecting oneself and others

Data protection and subject access rights

The Archbishops' Council, after liaison with dioceses and with the Data Protection Commissioner's office, has issued a guide about the Data Protection Act and its implication for churches. It includes an explanation of the term 'notification', which used to be known as 'registration' and is the process whereby each person or body regarded as a 'data controller' informs the Data Protection Commissioner (DPC) that they are handling personal data. Incumbents and PCCs are considered to be data controllers, as they are both separate legal entities and will be processing personal data. PCCs should be exempt from notification as all they are likely to hold are parochial records for the normal administration of the parish, and incumbents (or priests-in-charge) should only need to notify if records of pastoral care discussions (that is, information relating to beliefs, relationships and opinions, etc., rather than purely factual information, such as date of birth, date of baptism, etc.) are held on computer. There is no need to notify if all the data is kept on paper-based files.

If you think you need to notify, you should phone the DPC notification helpline (01625 545740). You will be asked some questions and then sent a form to complete and return, together with a fee of £35 currently (payable annually).

Even if the PCC and/or incumbent is exempt from notification, the remainder of the Act still applies to them and to everyone in the parish who handles personal data.

The Act sets out eight principles under which personal data may be obtained, held or disclosed to others:

1 The use of the data must be fair and lawful.
2 The information must be used only for specified purposes.

(Individuals should be informed, in broad terms, what you are going to do with the information.)

3 The information should be relevant and not excessive in relation to the purpose for which it is to be used.

4 The information must be accurate and up to date. You should periodically check that all the information held is still accurate.

5 Information should be kept for no longer than is necessary for its purpose. (Records of pastoral care discussions, for example, should not be kept for several years unless there is a particular justifiable reason for doing so.)

6 Individuals' access rights to the data must be honoured.

7 The information must be kept securely. Addresses and telephone numbers should not be left where unauthorized people could get hold of them, and access to other and more sensitive information should be particularly restricted by the use of computer passwords or locked filing cabinets, as appropriate.

8 The information held should not be transferred to any country outside Europe without adequate data protection being in place. (This is unlikely to be a matter that affects the church, whereas it is clearly relevant to a company setting up a call centre in India.)

Two areas of application of the Data Protection Act should be mentioned: the electoral roll and applications for marriage. It is now generally agreed that it is not sensible, and may even be a violation of the Act, to display lists of names and addresses on the church notice-board. The Church Representation Rules 2004 require, however, that, after the completion of the annual revision, a copy of the roll is to be published 'by being exhibited continuously for not less than fourteen days . . . on or near the principal door of the parish church in such manner as the council [PCC] shall appoint' (Rule 2 (3)). To be useful to a parish, the electoral roll needs to contain names *and* addresses and indeed Rule 1 (11) states:

The roll shall where practicable contain a record of the address of every person whose name is entered on the roll, but a failure to comply with this requirement shall not prejudice the validity of any entry on the roll.

The purpose of the *display* of the roll is so that members may ascertain if they have been included on it as requested. It is not intended to be a parish directory where people can look up addresses. It is sufficient, therefore, to display the list of names. If some indication of address is needed to differentiate between people of similar name, then a postcode could be printed rather than a full address. In general, churches should not encourage 'sign-up lists' that ask for names with addresses or telephone numbers, as it makes it possible for someone to use the data for non-church purposes.

The clergy need basic information about those they are marrying, both to discharge the legal requirements of a wedding (banns and registers) and pastorally (to make prayers and address appropriate). A priest (or administrator/secretary, as appropriate) should explain to the couple what use will be made of the information that is being given. If one of the couple has a spouse still living by a former marriage, the priest will require further information. After a decision has been made about a wedding, this material should be destroyed. Once the information needed has been recorded in the registers and the wedding has taken place, the application forms and notes should be destroyed.

A shredder is a vital part of church office equipment today, and it is a good principle to ensure that nothing carrying a name, address, telephone number or other personal data leaves the office in a refuse bag unless it has first been shredded. It is also sensible to shred parish financial data such as duplicate statements or interim financial reports rather than just throwing them away.

Since 24 October 2001 individuals have had the right to access information held about them ('personal data') within 40 days of making a request to see it. Data controllers may charge a fee of up to £10 for providing the information. This covers all information held on computer and any correspondence or other papers from which it could be considered relatively easy to extract relevant information, provided that the information is in what is termed a 'relevant filing system'. It is *not* necessary to provide actual copies of letters or other documents.

The Information Commissioner issued a clarification of two issues raised in the case of Durant v. Financial Services Authority, which was determined in the Court of Appeal on 8 December 2003. The issues were:

1 What makes 'data' personal within the meaning of 'personal data'?
2 What is meant by a 'relevant filing system'?

The Court of Appeal concluded that personal data is: 'Information that affects [a person's] privacy, whether in his personal or family life, business or professional capacity.'

The Commissioner concluded that:

> The concept of privacy is therefore clearly central to the definition of personal data. This suggests to the Commissioner that you should take into account whether or not the information in question is capable of having an adverse impact on the individual. The Court identified two notions that may assist in determining whether information 'is information that affects [an individual's] privacy':

> > 'The first is whether the information is biographical in a significant sense, that is, going beyond the recording of [the individual's] involvement in a matter or an event which has no personal connotations . . .'

> The second concerns focus.

> > 'The information should have the [individual] as its focus rather than some other person with whom he may have been involved or some transaction or event in which he may have figured or have had an interest . . .'

And the Commissioner carried on to say:

> Where an individual's name appears in information the name will only be 'personal data' where its inclusion in the information affects the named individual's privacy. Simply because an individual's name appears on a document, the information contained in that document will not necessarily be personal data about the named individual.

> It is more likely that an individual's name will be 'personal data' where the name appears together with other information about the named individual such as address, telephone number or information regarding his hobbies.

The Commissioner's comments on a 'relevant filing system' are lengthy (and can be read at <http://www.informationcommissioner.gov.uk>) but there is one piece of reassurance for ecclesiastical authorities who receive subject access notices:

> following the Durant judgment it is likely that very few manual files will be covered by the provisions of the DPA. Most information about individuals held in manual form does not, therefore, fall within the data protection regime.

The Commissioner provides a quick guide to 'relevant filing systems':

1 Does your filing system contain information about any individuals?
   Yes – go to Q 2.
   No – you do not have a 'relevant filing system'.
2 Does the filing system use the names of individuals (or another unique identifier) as the file name?
   Yes – go to Q 4.
   No – go to Q 3.
3 Does the filing system use criteria relating to individuals (e.g. sickness absence, pensions, or qualifications) as the file name?
   Yes – go to Q 4.
   No – you do not have a 'relevant filing system'.
4 Is the information in your files held solely in chronological order?
   Yes – you do not have a 'relevant filing system'.
   No – go to Q 5.
5 Is the content of your files indexed or subdivided to allow direct access to specific information about the individual?
   Yes – you are likely to have a 'relevant filing system'.
   No – you do not have a 'relevant filing system'.

James Behrens, Chancellor of the Diocese of Leicester, discussed the implications of the Data Protection Act 1998 in his article 'No Secrets in the Church',[15] but his comments and concerns must be read in the light of this new guidance. It can now be argued that a general parochial paper-based file kept about a member of staff or a candidate for ordination, which is not divided up into personal information, references, etc., is not part of a 'relevant filing system'. Behrens makes the point that a file of *complaints* about an incumbent is there 'to give the bishop specific information about the complaints made about that incumbent' and so is a 'relevant filing system'.

If you do have a 'relevant filing system', then you must disclose the material to an applicant. Behrens gives two principles: 'The first is that in responding to a subject access request, you do not normally need to name names. The second is that in general you must provide all the information you have about the data subject, unless it would require disproportionate effort to do so.'

After reading this section, you may think that you would like to know what personal data the bishop, archdeacon and rural dean have about you. You can do this, if it seems desirable, by serving a Subject Access Notice on them. This can be done by writing a letter stating that you require access, as permitted by the Data Protection Act, and wish to know what personal data about you is being held by them. You should send the necessary fee (currently £10) and remind them that the Act requires them to comply promptly and, at any event, in not more than 40 days from receiving the access notice. If you don't receive the information by the expiration of the period, you should remind them of their obligations and of your intention to contact the office of the Data Protection Commissioner. They are permitted, of course, to withhold information concerning any serious allegation against you as long as they are using that data in ways governed by other legislation, e.g. the Ecclesiastical Jurisdiction Measure, and revealing the information would compromise the inquiry. If you discover, on receiving the data, that the archdeacon, by way of example, is keeping the correspondence regarding a complaint made about you five or six years ago, then you may ask what the justification is for its retention, i.e. is it being kept longer than necessary? The archdeacon will probably reply that he has a duty to inform the bishop if a pattern of complaint emerges, e.g. people write to him or her every year or so complaining that you were rude to them.

James Behrens believes that files kept for the purpose of clergy discipline concerning dishonesty, seriously improper conduct, unfitness or incompetence on the part of the clergy 'will in most cases be covered by an exemption for those involved in regulatory activity'. This exemption should cover the preliminary stages of the disciplinary process as well as the proceedings themselves, and would cover 'peripheral' stages if subject access rights would be likely to prejudice the process. 'Likely to prejudice' must, in the Commissioner's view, mean that 'there would have to be a substantial chance rather than a mere risk that in a particular case the purposes would be noticeably damaged'. This exemption apart, Behrens thinks that, if a bishop is any good at administration, the bishop's files will constitute a 'relevant filing system' and he must permit the right of subject access.

Behaviour

A high standard of behaviour is expected from all, ordained or lay, who minister to people in situations of weakness. It is now generally acknowledged that an imbalance of power creates the possibility of exploitation and abuse. Ministers must guard against this and particularly when dealing with sick people be careful to allow them their full and proper dignity, accepting their reserve in matters relating to their sickness, and respecting their physical persons. Care must be taken over language, gesture and touch. Only the highest possible standards will maintain the high regard that the faithful have for their ministers and prevent scandal. As a basic rule, the minister should always dress appropriately – e.g. neither in sports kit nor dressed for a cocktail party. In an emergency it may be necessary to make a call on a sick person in casual clothes but this should be exceptional.

Be wary of letting down your guard accidentally – if, for instance, you have been drinking.

Pastoral care should always take place in ordinary circumstances and never be concealed or be at odd times or places. It is as well to establish expectations about what is normal pastoral behaviour by discussing it within the parish and by teaching about what ministry to the sick involves. If there is any doubt, ask whether something is acceptable. Better still, if you have any doubts about or difficulties with a particular situation, ask another person to be present, though possibly at a discreet distance. It is always better to be safe.

The Diocese of London's Regulations and Policies include the following list of basic precautions under the heading 'Clergy Safety':

- Ensure other people know when you are seeing people.
- Do not leave unknown visitors unattended in your office or house.
- Do not invite unknown visitors beyond the office or the study in your house.
- Do not see children alone (this is likely in any event to be prohibited by your parish's Child Protection Policy).
- Ensure porches and entrances are well lit; use spy-holes and chains on doors.

Policies

We have already noted in *Churchwardens: A Survival Guide* the importance of putting various policies in place, to protect oneself and others, in this increasingly litigious age. We have provided examples of model policies in the areas of insurance,[16] child protection,[17] fire precautions,[18] risk management[19] and disability access,[20] and we would refer you to that book for further information in those areas.

The most important thing is to be informed about relevant current legislation and implement it, ensuring all necessary policies are in place, regularly updated and actually adhered to. Policies and legislation concerning employees and volunteers will be surveyed in the next chapter.

It is sensible to maintain an accident and/or incident book in which are recorded any accidents or incidents necessitating any kind of treatment (particularly, but not only, accidents involving children). The date of the accident should be put in the book, along with the names of those concerned and of those involved in the treatment or necessary action. The record of the incident should then be signed and dated by the adult in charge. The book should be kept in perpetuity as the information would be vital in the event of any subsequent insurance claim.

Stress

Stress is simply the body's non-specific response to any demand made on it. Stress is not by definition synonymous with nervous tension or anxiety. Stress provides the means to express talents and energies and pursue happiness; it can also cause exhaustion and illness, either physical or psychological; heart attacks and accidents.[21]

Stress is the adverse reaction people have to excessive pressure. It isn't a disease. But if stress is intense and goes on for some time, it can lead to mental and physical ill health (e.g. depression, nervous breakdown, heart disease).[22]

Burnout refers to a state of physical, emotional and mental exhaustion that results from long-term involvement with people in emotionally demanding situations. Symptoms include stereotyped behaviour, emotional deadness, loss of interest in 'clients' and blaming them for their predicament, withdrawal from colleagues, and loss of a sense of meaning and purpose.[23]

Clergy are often put under pressure as they try to meet the many and varied demands of ministry but when demands and pressures become excessive and exceed the individual's ability to cope, then they lead to stress. Employers have a duty in law to ensure that employees are not made ill by their work. As the clergy have no employer, they need to take responsibility themselves for reducing the stress they experience. What are the outward signs of stress? The most obvious are changes in mood and behaviour, including lack of concentration, deteriorating relationships with others, irritability, indecisiveness, apathy or depression, and reduced performance. People who are stressed turn to comfort eating, to cigarettes, to increased alcohol consumption and perhaps to use of drugs of various sorts, including sleeping tablets. They may experience anxiety for no specific reason and feel a knot in the stomach. Among other indicators are:

- excessive tiredness;
- elevated heart rate;
- increased blood pressure;
- increased accident proneness;
- trembling;
- insomnia;
- migraines and headaches;

- skin problems;
- lower back pain;
- neck pain;
- changes in appetite and sleep pattern.

What causes stress? Well, the answers given by most consultants are not good news for the majority of clergy (see Alan Chapman's account on <http://www.businessballs.com>):

- continuous unreasonable performance demands;
- too much to do, too little time;
- lack of effective communication and conflict resolution;
- lack of control over work activities;
- lack of job security;
- lack of support from superiors and others;
- long working hours;
- a culture of blame and complaint;
- a feeling that one's reward is not commensurate with one's responsibility;
- persistent financial worries.

But the good news is that clergy are, on the whole, healthier and live longer than their peers. We are not, however, immune from stress and there is a significant and growing incidence of clergy burnout.

Stress is a process that builds and we need to be aware of growing stress and do something about it. There is plenty of advice to be found on the web, in books, and through courses. One stress management consultancy – Illumine Training of Windsor (see <http://www.illumine.co.uk/managing-stress.htm>) – offers seven tips for managing and avoiding harmful stress based on the word NURTURE:

N – nutrition
U – understand causes
R – realistic expectations
T – thinking
U – under control
R – relaxation
E – exercise and environment

These seven headings encapsulate most of the advice available.

Nutrition

Breakfast is important; we should drink more water and less coffee, unless it is decaffeinated; snacks should be healthy, meals well balanced, avoiding fats, processed food and refined sugars, but with plenty of fruit and vegetables. We should reduce alcohol intake and take time to eat.

Understand causes

Why are we stressed? Much of it arises from a needless effort to secure the goodwill and approval of others. Time and task management is vital. Be aware when other factors – especially illness (of self or others), bereavement, and relationship problems – are added to those caused by ministry. Examine work pressures. Don't set out to make dramatic and radical changes; small but important modifications can be very significant in reducing stress.

Realistic expectations

Don't simply do what you (or your predecessors) have always done because 'it has always been done that way'. We are no longer in the one priest/one parish/one church situation and we need to adapt accordingly.

Thinking

Consider the ways in which you think – negative thoughts deplete your energy; teach yourself to think positively – the cup is half full, not half empty.

Under control

No one is immune to stress; look at your coping strategies, and consider changing how you think about things; think of different ways of responding to pressures.

Relaxation

This ranges from prayer, meditation and daydreaming through hobbies and collecting to going for a walk, reading a book, stroking the cat, or taking a bath. Relaxation times mustn't be just what is left over; you have to plan for leisure.

Exercise and environment

Make physical activity a part of everyday life; walk rather than drive; play a sport, go to the pool, join a gym and use it. Be aware of the space around you, especially your office or study – keep it clear and organized.

We have also noticed bits of advice that don't fit into the seven headings but are worth noting (some of them come from a leaflet 'Basic Rules for Avoiding Stress' by Prof. H. R. Beech and Dr E. L. Teasdale, issued by ICI in 1988 – showing that the problem is not a new one – and from another stress management website, <http://www.mindtools.com/stress>).

- Smile and laugh.
- Be tidy and orderly. Untidiness tends to create a sense of time urgency.
- Get up a few minutes earlier and just 'potter' around, allowing yourself time to wake up and prepare for the day.
- Learn to say 'No'! You need to say 'no' to commitments that, if taken on, would cause intense stress and exhaustion.
- Be aware that it is not possible to do some jobs.
- Don't rush around frantically; pace yourself.
- Remember all areas of your life are important, not just work.
- Don't set out to win everything.
- Don't procrastinate.
- Don't talk too much; don't monopolize conversation; listen to others.
- Try to avoid getting impatient.
- Don't be put out when things go wrong.
- Make sure you get enough sleep.
- Remember to plan for and take your days off and holiday.

Clergy are no different from those working in other professions in being reluctant to admit that they are feeling stressed. This is because we see 'being stressed' as a sign of weakness. It is actually failure to deal with stress that is a weakness.

♦ 5 ♦

Working with others:
Employees and volunteers

What is an employee?

The employment of others is, alas, a minefield, but there are steps that can be taken to minimize the risks involved and to increase the possibility of positive benefits to all concerned. A useful working definition of 'employee' can be found in a report produced by the Diocese of Blackburn entitled *Employment of Lay Workers: Guidelines for Parishes* and available at their website <http://www.blackburn.anglican.org/index.htm>: 'an individual who works in a parish and receives some form of remuneration from the parish (either honorarium, hourly wage or salary) and who is employed by the PCC'. It is important to be aware that a contract of service exists once an employer and employee have agreed upon the terms and conditions of the employment, even if the agreement is not in writing.

This chapter is concerned with the parish's lay employees. Any stipendiary assistant clergy working in the parish – who are legally grouped under the term 'assistant curates' even if the term 'associate vicar', 'associate rector', or 'associate minister' is used – are licensed by the bishop and not employed by the PCC. The terms under which the licence is issued are governed by Canon C 12. It can be a general licence to minister in any parish or a licence to perform some particular office and, for an 'assistant curate', for a specified term of years. The bishop may 'for any cause which appears to him to be good and reasonable' revoke a licence 'summarily, and without further process' after giving due notice of the possibility of appeal to the archbishop. If implemented, the recommendations of the McClean Review of Clergy Terms of Service will grant greater security of tenure and access to Employment Tribunals, but this is not the case at present.

If the church is to be a good employer it is essential that employment legislation be adhered to (the Employment Rights Act 1996 is the key piece of legislation here), that financial arrangements be robust and understood, and that the PCC, as the employer, fully understands its responsibilities. Help and advice are available from ACAS and a useful publication is *The Good Employment Guide for the Voluntary Sector*, published by the National Council for Voluntary Organisations (NCVO).

Recruitment

The first aspect to consider is the recruitment process. Prior to advertising a post the PCC should ideally have drawn up and agreed an Equal Opportunities Policy. A form of words could be as follows:

> Recruitment, selection, training, and consideration for promotion for those who work within our organization are available to all without unfair discrimination, and we will work to ensure that no one is disadvantaged in any of these matters by conditions and requirements that cannot be shown to be justifiable. We will work to ensure that there is no discrimination on the grounds of race, colour, nationality (including citizenship), ethnic or national origins, disability, age, gender, married or single status, where any of these cannot be shown to be a requirement of the job and office concerned.

If the person appointed will be required to go through the Criminal Records Bureau (CRB) Disclosure process, this needs to be stated in any advertisement or other recruitment literature.

Prior to recruitment the PCC also needs to have drawn up and agreed a job description for the post. A clear job description can prevent all kinds of difficulties arising in the future, such as misunderstandings about who does what, who reports to whom, where one person's job ends and another's begins. A job description is also an essential tool for management, in reviewing an employee's work, assessing training needs, and deciding whether a role needs to be developed. Alongside the job description there should be a person specification, describing the kind of experience, qualifications, talents and personal qualities likely to be present in the ideal candidate for the job. Job description and person specification should naturally fit together. The job description should state if there is to be a probationary period and how long it will be. The PCC should decide how many referees will be required, what categories they might fall into (present employer, a priest, etc.), and whether references should be requested from the candidate at the time of application or at the time of shortlisting or be requested by the PCC prior to or after interview. This will determine the interview and appointment timescale (i.e. more time must be allowed before interview if references must be received by then).

The advertisement – in the *Church Times*, *Church of England Newspaper* or other appropriate publication – should briefly indicate the nature of the position, remuneration, accommodation (if provided), closing date for applications, date for interview, date for commencement, and the way in which further information can be obtained (website or other address; a telephone number or email address encourages enquiry by those means). The material sent to enquirers should give the timetable in full: applications by, shortlisting on, interviews on, start date. Those responsible for the interview process must stick to this timetable and notify people promptly if they have not been shortlisted or appointed. The PCC should agree on the make-up of the shortlisting and interview panels and consider whether there should be an outside interviewer (e.g. someone from the diocese, someone with Human Resources (HR) skills).

The selection process is not easy and can be full of pitfalls. The shortlisting panel should carefully read all the applications and check them against the criteria for appointment. Those who clearly don't fit at all should be notified that they have not been shortlisted. A shortlist of between three and six candidates should be agreed, depending on the strength of the field. A programme for the day or half-day should be drawn up, offering candidates a chance to see the church, school, parish plant and facilities, accommodation, etc., as appropriate, depending on the position being filled. The order of interviewing may depend on travel times, otherwise it can be determined by drawing names out of a hat. The interview panel should agree a list of questions and put them to each of the shortlisted candidates, endeavouring to find the closest match between the individuals interviewed and the person specification. If the person needs to have certain skills (e.g. computer skills or, in the case of a musician, organ and conducting skills), there should be an opportunity for these to be tested or demonstrated. Do not be afraid not to appoint if no one comes near the requirements of the person specification. It is better to have an unfilled post than an employment disaster. And if you do appoint someone (after taking up references), and they seem perfect in every respect, still make sure that you have a probationary period in place and that you stick with it.

More often in the church than in other organizations, someone just emerges to fill a job, often from the congregation, without advertisement or formal interview procedure. In these cases you should still ensure a properly agreed job description and remuneration package are drawn up and implemented, and have a CV and references on file.

As mentioned above, certain posts carry with them the necessity of CRB Disclosure before the new employee can be confirmed in post. These include posts of people who will be working with children (compulsory) and posts requiring handling of money (advisable). Standard Disclosure is primarily for positions that involve working with children or regular contact with vulnerable adults. It contains details of all convictions on record (including spent convictions) and details of any cautions, reprimands or warnings. For positions involving working with children, Standard Disclosure will also give any information contained in government department lists of people considered unsuitable to work with children. Enhanced Disclosure is applicable to positions that involve regularly caring for, training, supervising, or being in sole charge of children or vulnerable adults. It involves an extra level of checking with local police records in addition to checks with the Police National Computer and government department lists, where appropriate. Your diocesan authorities will have systems in place for how the disclosure is managed, but further information can be obtained from the Criminal Records Bureau website at <http://www.crb.gov.uk>. The Disclosure service run by the CRB is at <http://www.disclosure.gov.uk/index.asp>.

Contracts of employment

In addition to the job description and person specification, a contract of employment needs to be drawn up; this will be signed by the employee and by somebody on behalf of the PCC (probably the incumbent as chairman of the PCC) once the appointment has been made. The contract should specify the terms and conditions of employment, including the rate of pay (which must, of course, be at least equal to the national minimum wage), holiday entitlement (specifying if it has to be taken in certain units and if it cannot be taken at certain times, e.g. Holy Week), and overtime arrangements, if any. Other terms and conditions which should be covered in the contract include the circumstances in which deductions may be made from wages (there are very limited circumstances in which this may happen, such as when a loan has been made to an employee by an employer and repayments are deducted from wages), time off work for public duties and other matters, suspension from work on health and safety grounds, arrangements for sick pay, maternity and paternity rights, termination of employment, grounds for dismissal, and redundancy. You should have a clear policy on the payment of legitimate expenses associated with the post and a means of accounting for them. You also need agreed procedures for induction, grievances and discipline.

If you are employing someone for the first time, you will also have to get to grips with deducting tax and National Insurance contributions from their pay, as well as making the employer's contribution to National Insurance. Information is available from your local Inland Revenue office, from the New Employers' helpline (Tel.: 0845 60 70 143) and from the Inland Revenue's website at <http://www.inlandrevenue.gov.uk/employers/index.shtml>. Information on pensions is available from the Pension Service at <http://www.thepensionservice.gov.uk>.

Job descriptions should be reviewed on a regular basis, at least once a year, and amendments should be made in the light of experience, changing circumstances, and the particular strengths and weaknesses of the employee. The review and the revised job description that emerges from it should be used to enable the employer and the employee to meet the developing needs of the organization (in this case, the church) and of one another, and you should not feel that the description is set in stone. Job descriptions should not be allowed to gather dust in a filing cabinet; they are tools to be used by employer and employee alike.

In addition to the contract of employment, it may be useful for the main rules of the organization to be provided in written form to all employees. These may take the form of a 'code of conduct'. The NCVO advises that the rules should be stated clearly in order to avoid any misunderstandings, and that special care should be taken to ensure all employees entering the working environment for the first time understand them. The rules, or code of conduct, may include examples of the sort of behaviour which would constitute gross misconduct and therefore lead to summary dismissal.

Employment legislation

The Employment Rights Act 1996 requires employers to provide their employees with details of what to do in the event of having a grievance, including specifying the person whom employees should approach. In addition, as a matter of good practice, it is recommended that a grievance policy be drawn up, adopted by the PCC and given to the employee. A grievance policy should state that employees must be given a fair hearing concerning any grievance they may have, and that they have a right to be accompanied by a colleague or trade union official when raising a grievance.

The kinds of issues concerning which an employee may feel he or she has a grievance which affects their well-being and thus their ability to carry out their work effectively include harassment, intimidation, bullying, incompetent colleagues, a dangerous work environment, a lack of resources to do the job properly, or too great a workload. To address these matters before they arise, the PCC may wish to draw up specific grievance policies covering particular areas of concern, such as sexual harassment or bullying. Such policies should clearly define the type of behaviour prohibited by them and spell out the disciplinary consequences of indulging in such behaviour.

It is important that employers take grievances and complaints seriously. If they are not addressed properly, an employee may feel he or she is unable to go on working for you. If they have been employed by you for more than a year they could, on resignation, make a claim for constructive dismissal as a result of the employer's inaction. (Any claim for constructive dismissal must be brought within three months of the employee's resignation.) Complaints of unfair dismissal or discrimination, or various other employment matters such as breach of contract, can, unless resolved by the parties involved, be heard by Employment Tribunals, which may order reinstatement or compensation. The right to a hearing on a complaint of unfair dismissal applies only to workers who have been employed for more than 12 months. (Should you be unfortunate enough to find yourself embroiled in a dispute of this sort, do remember to check your insurance policy as you may find it covers you for at least some of the costs involved.)

Other legislation affecting employers and employees includes the Equal Pay Act 1970, the Rehabilitation of Offenders Act 1974, the Children Act 1989 (sometimes referred to – erroneously – as the Child Protection Act 1989), the Sex Discrimination Act 1975, the Race Relations Act 1976, the Employment Equality Regulations 2003, the Health and Safety at Work Act 1974, the Management of Health and Safety at Work Regulations 1999, the Disability Discrimination Act 1995, the Working Time Regulations 1998, the Data Protection Act 1998 and the Fire Precautions (Workplace) Regulations 1997. Each of these is looked at in turn, very briefly in some cases.

The Equal Pay Act 1970

This requires employers to pay men and women an equal wage when the work they do is of equal value.

The Rehabilitation of Offenders Act 1974

This states that job applicants do not have to reveal that they are former offenders if they have been sentenced to no more than 30 months' imprisonment and have served a period of rehabilitation. For certain jobs, however – particularly for those which include work with young people under the age of 18 – there is no rehabilitation period and past convictions must be declared.

The Children Act 1989

The House of Bishops has stated that the Church of England accepts the principle enshrined in the Children Act 1989 that the welfare of the child is paramount. A PCC policy on child protection, though tailored to the needs of the local parish, must be based on the recommendations of the *Church of England House of Bishops' Policy on Child Protection* and any guidelines issued by the diocese (each diocese may have its own variations), as well as meeting the requirements stated under the Act and the Home Office's guidelines. Staff and volunteers dealing with children will need to be properly recruited, trained and supported. They will also need to be familiarized with the Church's Policy on Child Protection, the *Church of England House of Bishops' Policy on Child Protection* and the diocesan guidelines. The PCC must also ensure that it has adequate insurance cover, including public liability insurance, for all activities organized by the church and held at the church that involve children. (The Children Act 1989 defines a child as a person under 18 for most purposes.) For an example of a policy statement for the protection of children and young people see pp. 80–1 of our book *Churchwardens: A Survival Guide*.

The Sex Discrimination Act 1975

This is concerned with both direct and indirect discrimination. Direct discrimination is when an employee has been treated less favourably than another in similar circumstances on the grounds of gender. Indirect discrimination occurs when a requirement is applied equally to male and female employees, but one gender is unable to comply. The most common example of indirect discrimination is a requirement for full-time working, which generally fewer women than men can do by reason of their child-care commitments. In these circumstances, the test tends to be whether the employer can justify their requirement for full-time work.

The Race Relations Act 1976

This is also concerned with both direct and indirect discrimination.

The Employment Equality Regulations 2003

The Employment Equality (Sexual Orientation) Regulations 2003 and the Employment Equality (Religion or Belief) Regulations 2003 which came into force on 1 and 2 December 2003 respectively outlaw discrimination in employment or vocational training on the grounds of sexual orientation and religion or belief, and are therefore of particular concern to church and other Christian organizations. The Archbishops' Council has produced a paper on the implementation of the Regulations; the Gloucester diocesan website usefully reproduces it at <http://www.glosdioc.org.uk/Home/EmpEq.pdf>. Both sets of Regulations do allow for exceptions in the case of a 'genuine occupational requirement' (GOR), but the Archbishops' Council does point out that a blanket policy of requiring all workers to be Christians or Anglicans will no longer be sustainable under these regulations which 'require an employer to show that affiliations of religion or belief are proportionate in relation to the particular post in question'. These regulations are not something to be frightened of but to be aware of when drawing up job descriptions and recruitment advertisements, which should 'clearly but sensitively state the position of the place of worship, parish or diocese on any requirement it imposes'. The Archbishops' Council makes the point, for instance, that 'some PCCs may conclude that it is proportionate to insist that a Christian should fill a particular secretarial or administrative post because it includes a local representational role for the Church with substantial contact with the public and a pastoral dimension'. A sexual orientation GOR is bound to be harder (though not necessarily impossible) to justify than a religion or belief one.

The Health and Safety at Work Act 1974
(and *The Management of Health and Safety at Work Regulations 1999)*

These require employers to provide and maintain a safe working environment and safe systems at work. It also requires them to ensure that non-employees, such as visitors, are not endangered by work activities, and that employees are trained in how to ensure a safe working environment. As the Ecclesiastical Insurance Group

(EIG, see <http://www.ecclesiastical.co.uk>) points out, churches present a vast range of health and safety issues, from food handling to working at high levels (or to the trip hazards of an uneven floor). Local Authority Environmental Health Officers are responsible for enforcing health and safety legislation in churches, as elsewhere. They have the power to enter a church at any time to ensure that you are complying with the law.

The law states that where you have five or more employees you must have a written health and safety policy, but it still makes sense to have one even if you have fewer than five employees. EIG is willing to make available to all parishes, free of charge, a detailed draft Health and Safety Policy. It can be obtained by attending a seminar run by an Ecclesiastical Insurance Consultant and Surveyor. The seminars last about an hour and are specifically designed to help you get to grips with health and safety issues.

EIG suggests that you appoint a particular individual to take overall responsibility for health and safety, and possibly set up a sub-committee or working party of the PCC to deal with these issues. EIG also offers a round-the-clock advice line if you have any enquiries regarding health and safety or employment law. The number is 0117 934 2104.

The Disability Discrimination Act 1995

This applies only to those who employ 15 or more people. It could nevertheless reasonably be considered good practice for the church to make an effort to recruit disabled workers and to make reasonable provision for them to be able to do their work.

The Working Time Regulations 1998

This places a statutory limit on working hours for most employees. It also requires employers to provide paid holiday, breaks and minimum rest periods.

The Data Protection Act 1998

This has been dealt with in the previous chapter.

The Fire Precautions (Workplace) Regulations 1997

When the church building is also a workplace (e.g. the parish office is located in the building or you have a verger or bookstall attendant working in the church), you need to comply with these regulations which include the following provisions: '(a) a workplace shall, to the extent that is appropriate, be equipped with appropriate fire-fighting equipment and with fire detectors and alarms; and (b) any non-automatic fire-fighting equipment so provided shall be easily accessible, simple to use and indicated by signs.' One or more employees will need to be given responsibility for fire-fighting and for training other employees. Churches which are also workplaces are subject to inspection by the local fire brigade to ensure that the regulations are being complied with; in the case of non-compliance, the fire brigade can serve an enforcement notice. (Even if the church is not used as a workplace, it does of course make good sense to have fire extinguishers in place, fire exits clearly marked and sidesmen trained in fire-fighting and evacuation procedures. For an example of a fire policy, see pp. 82–3 of our book *Churchwardens: A Survival Guide.*)

The use of volunteers

You may by now be thinking you will do best to avoid employing people altogether, and rely instead on volunteers. There are, however, pitfalls to be avoided here too! In particular, you need to take care that you do not inadvertently treat your volunteers as employees, and thus lay the way open for a disgruntled ex-volunteer to make a claim with the Employment Tribunals for unfair dismissal. A particularly useful resource on both employment and volunteer issues is 'askNCVO', an online best practice resource for the voluntary sector, maintained by the National Council for Voluntary Organisations (NCVO) and accessible from their website at <http://www.ncvo-vol.org.uk/>.

There is currently no legislation specifically covering volunteer workers, nor is there any legal definition of who constitutes a volunteer worker. There are certain things you should be careful of in order to ensure volunteers do not become employees in the eyes of the law. For instance, though volunteers may welcome – and indeed require – training, any agreement you have with a volunteer should not characterize training as a right. Instead, the agreement can express the intention of training being offered when and where possible in order to help the volunteer carry out his or her particular role effectively. Training should be given only when it can be seen to be directly related to the work the volunteer is doing. Furthermore, an organization is not entitled to require anything from its volunteers, such as a minimum time commitment, in return for training. Binding arrangements of this sort have been ruled by the courts to constitute a contract of employment.

Though it is safer to avoid 'contracts' for volunteers, which can lead to false expectations of obligation on both sides, it is nevertheless good practice to have a written agreement. This can include a role description (note not 'job' description) and it can help both parties to clarify their intentions and expectations. In order to avoid an 'agreement' becoming a 'contract', it is important not to write about, or imply, the existence of rights and obligations. Instead you should concentrate on such concepts as intentions, hopes or policies, thus reflecting the voluntary nature of the arrangement. Likewise, though it is good practice to reimburse volunteers for expenses they have incurred while working for you, the safest option is to reimburse only actual expenses, preferably against receipts. To pay an 'expenses' per diem, automatically, can be seen in tribunals as the equivalent of paying a salary (albeit a very small one). Examples of legitimate expenses which may be paid to volunteers include:

- travel to and from the place of volunteering;
- travel undertaken in the course of volunteering;
- meals taken during the course of volunteering;
- postage and telephone costs if the volunteer is working from home;
- protective clothing or other essential equipment;
- childcare expenses.

Despite the necessity of ensuring volunteers do not accidentally become employees, there are certain aspects of employment and other legislation which necessarily cover volunteers too. Chief among these is the requirement of all volunteers who will be working with children or vulnerable adults to go through the CRB Disclosure process, just like any employee working in those areas. Volunteers also need to be fully covered by appropriate insurance: they, just like paid staff, may face risks of personal injury, liability for accidents, and loss of or damage to property. An organization will also be liable for the negligent actions of its volunteers (such as the provision of incorrect advice or allowing visitors into dangerous parts of a building) and needs to ensure that the public is protected. Ecclesiastical Insurance reports that the Health and Safety Executive is increasingly viewing volunteers as employees and expects them to be provided with the same level of protection.

The NCVO provides the following checklist covering all aspects of volunteer management:

1 Write a volunteering strategy.
2 Write volunteering policies.
3 Write a role description and role specification for each volunteer vacancy.
4 Ensure you have relevant references and CRB checks for each volunteer.
5 Induct all new volunteers and those taking on a new or increased role.
6 Provide training relevant to the volunteer's work or role.
7 Provide highly supportive supervision and management.
8 Ensure volunteer documents do not set out 'rights' or 'obligations'.

You may well feel it is depressing even to have to consider some of these issues, that in a community based on the love of God, there is no place for grievance, complaint, tribunals, dismissals and allegations. You want to believe that church volunteers are always upright, well-intentioned, and never neurotic people, and that someone applying to work in a church is equally blameless and selfless and would never dream of taking you to an employment tribunal. You would, however, be naive to think so – as any experience of working with the imperfect human beings we all are will surely tell you – and you would be seriously misguided to act on this naive belief and neglect to put all the correct policies in place. Forewarned is forearmed, and it is far better to take time over policies for grievance and discipline which may never have to be implemented than not to do so and find your good intentions have been taken advantage of and you are in a fix. It is also in the best interests of the church as an institution to be shown to be a good employer, exercising due care and consideration over its employees and volunteers as well as ensuring it is protected from inadequate or malicious workers.

You may also feel, however, somewhat aggrieved at being expected to treat your employees so nobly, while the employment status of the clergy remains a matter of some confusion and debate, and you yourself have at present no recourse to employment tribunals, protection from long working hours, difficult people and other grievances, or adequate management of any variety. Perhaps even the hierarchy of the Church of England will have to come into line with the rest of the world eventually. Meanwhile you need to work out your own strategies for how to survive.

♦ 6 ♦

How am I doing? Appraisal and review

Appraisal

The purpose of appraisal and review is growth within ministry.
Appraisal is normally a process carried out by the priest with the
aid and encouragement of an independent consultant. Review of
the priest's ministry is necessarily a part of an examination of the
totality of parish ministry undertaken by clergy and laity together.
These are only now becoming normal within the Church of
England. Appraisal, or external work consultancy, is more often to
be found than review, but remains optional in many dioceses.
Review, including evaluation of what has gone before, planning for
the medium-term future, and dreaming about the long-term future,
is intended to develop strong ministry and the central question is
'How well is this congregation or parish and its ordained leader
meeting God's and its own expectations of what can be achieved
in mutual ministry?' It is, of course, difficult to make anything
mandatory when there are, as yet, no sanctions to apply in the
event of failure to comply. The priest who cares about the work he
or she is doing will, however, want to ask the two basic questions
'How am I doing?' and 'How can I do what I am doing better?'

Appraisal should be conducted annually. A questionnaire may
provide the starting point, setting the scene for the consultant. A
longer statement may be needed initially or on changing consultants. If this is carried out as an entirely confidential procedure,
with only an agreed statement going to the bishop, then all papers
are returned to the priest, and all conversations remain confidential. The consultant needs to be a person with a good deal of experience of the church and its ministers and some knowledge of the
psychology of the clergy, who can facilitate a frank conversation
that enables the priest to review the achievements and failures of
the past year and to look a little way into the future. The annual

appraisal – which goes by different names in different dioceses (e.g. 'Ministerial review' in the Diocese of London) – is intended to look at change during the year. The London system asks questions under three headings: ministerial growth and development, personal growth and development, vision ('Do I have a vision upholding and guiding my ministry?') of the way forward.

The difficulty with this approach – necessary as it may be – is its focus on 'me'. As we have indicated already, ministry has never been about the priest operating in splendid isolation but about the priest in the church interacting with a variety of different people and bodies. Appraisal can be useful, but in the same way that the counsellor sees the problem through the eyes of the client and the psychotherapist through the eyes of the patient, so the consultant sees the parish through the eyes of the priest. The priest may reach the conclusion in the appraisal that he is not doing what he was trained to do or that she is not using the very gifts that first brought her to ordination. Appraisal as an isolated activity will not remedy this feeling and it needs to be complemented by a review of ministry that engages the parish and its representatives.

Review

A review undertaken within and with the parish requires realism from the lay participants who are involved in the life of the parish. When a priest ministers to a number of congregations or a number of parishes, the review process provides an opportunity to set realistic objectives that will need to be agreed by all the participating congregations and parishes. If you are to be more effective in ministry and to adapt to changed circumstances, you need to be aware of how people feel about the life of the church. It is not enough to listen to what is said to you at the church door after a service ('Another interesting sermon, vicar') or the reports that come to you from churchwardens and others ('People are saying . . .'). The former may make you feel good; the latter depressed. There are many ways of gaining feedback about how people feel about you, the church, and the activities that take place in the church. The PCC should, but hardly ever does, provide that sort of feedback. Church members often feel that they are not consulted, but do not themselves want to be involved in the actual business of running the church. A review process can provide an opportunity for them to be heard.

The review process could be annual, and the priest could use the material in self-appraisal with a consultant, but it need not be annual (and so become just another chore) and might instead mark various stages in the life of the parish, but at no more than three-year intervals. If things are going well, there will always be a temptation not to do a review at all. If there are any disappointments, on either side, the temptation is to use the review as an outlet for anger, frustration and criticism. Omitting an evaluation in happy times is almost always a mistake. When tension has developed, when there are problems, disagreements, protests and resignations, evaluation is not the issue. The issue is problem solving and we should fix the problem, not the blame.

The ideal starting point for the review process is the parish profile prepared by the PCC (or PCCs) and used by the bishop and the parish representatives in the appointment process, together with documentation provided by the priest as part of the appointment procedure, and any mission statement or action plan or objectives agreed by the PCC during the year. If the initial review process begins toward the end of the first year in a new parish, then many of the sorts of problems that mar a second year can be avoided and each year growth can be celebrated and encouraged. The review process is not – and must not become – an opportunity for the minister's critics to have a field day. It must have at least these four characteristics:

- A protective, supportive climate to help ministers deal with the personal dimensions that are involved in their work, and to face negative feedback, if necessary.
- Possibilities for developing growth, including the commitment of parish resources to aid continuing ministerial education.
- Opportunities of doing something about what is discovered or identified in the review process.
- Clear, measurable, achievable expectations.

A priest may well look at the outline of the review process and simply think 'Oh no! I am not giving them a chance to have a go at me.' Many clergy would share such sentiments but as we move into a different environment the clergy must not be passive. A first review, if it has not been begun until several years into a job, will undoubtedly require very careful preparation. Before suggesting it to a PCC, the priest will certainly want to feel confident that it will be conducted in a truly loving spirit and be directed towards the well-being of both priest and parish.

Some initial teaching will be necessary. Though we frequently explain the difference between the office of the priest and the responsibilities involved in being a rector, vicar, or priest-in-charge, the laity do not generally perceive the clear difference between role and responsibilities, between office and job. They will need to do so if our role as priests is not to be confused with, and submerged beneath, our responsibilities as incumbents or priests-in-charge. Priesting means being – being 'messengers, watchmen, and stewards of the Lord', as the ordinal puts it, feeding and providing for the Lord's family, searching for 'his children in the wilderness of this world's temptations', guiding them 'through its confusions, so that they may be saved through Christ for ever'. Vicaring means doing – planning services, arranging weddings and funerals, preparing for meetings, dealing with budgets and buildings. Priesting calls up words like mystery, faith, spirituality. Vicaring calls up words like professionalism, competence, responsibility. The priest belongs in church or among his or her people; the vicar belongs in the office. Development of ministry must embrace the whole of the person's vocation and ministry – role, responsibilities, and plans for the future.

The functions of the clergy as well as their pastoral specialities vary, as we know, very greatly and this means that any form of clergy appraisal or review must take into consideration both the common denominators for duties and competence (the 'core competences' in Human Resources jargon) and the specific demands of the position being occupied (i.e. the particular job in a particular place). Lay people involved in a review process need to be aware of these common denominators or core competences. The Church Deployment Board of the American Episcopal Church developed the idea of 'pastoral specialities' (by which they mean the common denominators rather than the requirements of a specific post) as 'one of the many devices which may be useful in naming and prioritizing the values and activities which priest and congregation

now find to be important in their mutual relationship'. They identified 17:

1   teacher of children: teach and work with pre-teenage children;
2   youth worker/teacher: teach and work with youth;
3   teacher of adults: teach and work with adults;
4   visitor: visit church members in their homes;
5   pastor: care for people so that they are nurtured and chal-
    lenged for growth within the community of faith;
6   crisis minister: respond to people at significant points in
    their lives e.g. death, dying, sickness, birth, trauma, success;
7   counsellor: assist, in a counselling setting, persons facing
    problems or decisions;
8   administrative leader: manage the affairs of the congrega-
    tion including programmes, organizations, finances, etc.;
9   evangelism leader: train and lead others in relating the
    Christian faith to the lapsed and to people outside the church;
10 ecumenical leader: participate in work with other denomina-
    tions or work sponsored jointly by a number of churches;
11 social ministry leader: enable persons within the congrega-
    tion to become aware of and participate in issues;
12 community leader: through personal involvement, to organize
    community groups to meet stated needs such as drug
    problems, decent housing, crime levels, discrimination, etc.;
13 stewardship leader: lead lay persons in the development and
    use of individual and congregational resources;
14 theologian: demonstrate a disciplined understanding of bibli-
    cal and historical revelation and the perception of God's
    activity in the world;
15 preacher: preach with clarity and make the Gospel relevant
    to people's lives;
16 liturgical leader: plan and conduct liturgical services of pub-
    lic worship;
17 spiritual guide/leader: lead and train others in the formation
    of a spiritual discipline.

These 'specialities' – and a priest may specialize in more than one,
and shift emphasis among them during the course of his or her ministry – combine many of the functions and duties of a priest that

are given in the ordinal. A frequent difficulty for priests is that they and/or the people to whom they minister imagine that a single priest is supposed to carry out all of these functions all of the time. This is clearly impossible, and to place such expectations on any person – or on oneself – will inevitably lead to a sense of failure at the very least, almost inevitably to stress and probably to burnout. It is important that in any review of a priest's performance it is clearly understood that he or she is not supposed to be exercising all of these functions, but that there should be mutual agreement, depending on the priest's particular gifts and the particular require-ments of the parish, as to which of these functions are currently expected to be to the fore. It should also be recognized that certain of these specialities will require that the priest be given the oppor-tunity for fresh input and training in order to keep up to date: ecumenical developments, for instance, are continually evolving, and a priest involved in counselling will need to be in supervision.

A further list to be considered in the review process is drawn from the 1980 ordinal and the canons. A priest is called:

- to work among people to whom he or she is sent as servant and shepherd;
- to work with the bishop and fellow priests;
- to proclaim the word of the Lord;
- to call people to repentance and to absolve them in Christ's name;
- to baptize;
- to prepare the baptized for confirmation;
- to preside at the celebration of the Holy Communion;
- to lead people in prayer and worship;
- to intercede for his or her people;
- to bless the people in the name of the Lord;
- to teach and encourage by word and example;
- to minister to the sick;
- to prepare the dying for death;
- to care for the people committed to his or her charge and to join them in a common witness to the world;
- to accept the discipline of the Church and give respect to those in authority;

- to be diligent in prayer, in reading holy Scripture and such other studies as pertain to ministerial duties;
- to fashion his or her own life according to the way of Christ;
- to make him- or herself a wholesome example and pattern to the flock of Christ;
- to promote unity, peace and love among all Christian people.

And a further list is of relevance to the parish priest. It is contained in the provisions of Canon C 24 'Of priests having a cure of souls' (there is some overlap here with lists we have given earlier):

- to say morning and evening prayer daily, and the litany when appointed, in church;
- to celebrate the Holy Communion on all Sundays and greater feast days, and Ash Wednesday (or to cause it to be celebrated);
- to diligently administer the sacraments and other rites of the Church;
- to preach, or cause to be preached, a sermon in church at least once every Sunday;
- to instruct the parishioners in the Christian faith;
- to use opportunities of teaching or visiting schools;
- to carefully prepare all such as desire to be confirmed and to present them to the bishop;
- to be diligent in visiting parishioners and especially the sick and infirm;
- to provide opportunities for parishioners to resort to him or her for spiritual counsel and advice;
- to consult with the PCC on matters of general concern and importance to the parish.

Yet another list could be drawn up of the matters to which the parish clergy must attend: participating in deanery chapter and synod, reading banns and issuing certificates, keeping registers, making returns to the registrar of marriages, completing, with the churchwardens and PCC secretary, returns to the diocese and archdeacon, ensuring faculties are applied for and complied with, chairing PCC meetings and annual meetings, making returns to the Church Commissioners, as well as completing and returning a tax return.

Suggested steps in the professional review of a priest

These steps have been expanded and developed from an outline in a publication – *Mutual Ministry Review: for Clergy and Parishes* – of the Church Deployment Board of the American Episcopal Church (1988).

1   **Develop a process**. The process must be appropriate for the local situation and for the participants. There are various models that can be used, and the parish does not have to invent a new one. It should choose an approach that fits the style of the review team and can be completed in the time available. The process must be mutually developed, considering the needs of both priest and parish or congregation. The needs of the parish may, of course, not be the same as those of the congregation. In addition the priest's ministry will generally include a number of contacts outside of the congregation but within the parish, and possibly some external to the parish. A review can helpfully look at the balance between congregational, parochial and extra-parochial ministry. The priest must be part of the process from the very beginning.

2   **Form a team**. The team is crucial to the success of the review. The whole team must thoroughly understand and trust the concept, style and objectives of the review process. The team should include three or four people apart from the priest. Ideally a consultant should be brought in to guide the process and the priest might also have an 'advocate' to join him or her. Review is an in-depth process and a small number of people forming the review team can help ensure that the process achieves its purpose and that feedback will be carefully and sensitively presented. Though the priest, as spiritual and temporal leader of the parish, may have overall responsibility for initiating and guiding the review, it is not necessary that he or she be involved in every detail of planning and administration. Priest and PCC can together select a lay person as head of the review team.

3   **Carry out an advance review**. This is an opportunity for each 'side' – priest and team – to consider separately what should

constitute the focus of the review and which areas of ministry require most scrutiny. Each should:

(a) revisit any previous reviews and the objectives that emerged from them;

(b) identify specific examples of typical performance in each area to be reviewed;

(c) agree on how to share data.

4 **Collect information.**

- Start with a look at what the priest has done in the last three months, tasks undertaken and time used for them. A calendar review usually provides indications of the content of ministry.

- Make a list of commonly held expectations: what do people expect of the priest? (It is not to be assumed that these expectations will necessarily be an accurate reflection of what the priest *ought* to be doing; i.e. the expectations may be unrealistic or based on a degree of ignorance.)

- Interview parishioners or use a survey asking 'When you think of the vicar of this parish, what qualities do you feel should be present?'

- Ask the rural or area dean, ministry team members, ecumenical colleagues and others for feedback.

The review team is looking for a consensus on the performance of the priest. It is all too often those who are critical of the priest who make their views known to the churchwardens (and copy them to the archdeacon and bishop!). The team will contribute their own observations and those from individuals with whom they have spoken. The most useful information will be current, typical, specific and identified.

- 'Current' means facts and figures which reflect recent events.

- 'Typical' is important because one out-of-character moment generally means little.

- 'Specific' refers to a certain moment, not a general statement.

- 'Identified' means that the source of the information is clearly known and not of the casual or mysterious nature

implied in statements like 'Some people are saying . . .' or
'Lots of people say . . .'.

5   **Priest's own report**. It should not be forgotten that the priest
   is an important source of data. By reviewing the foundational documents (ordinal, Canons, parish profile, mission action
   plan, etc.), the priest will identify areas of strength and weakness, achievements and failures. These too should be specific,
   typical, and current.

6   **Development discussion**. The priest and the review team
   bring together their reflections and they
   (a) discuss past objectives and responsibilities;
   (b) review performance and develop a common list of areas
        for further attention;
   (c) agree on objectives for the next period of a year or more;
   (d) agree ways to accomplish the objectives and the means of
        knowing when they have been accomplished.

This discussion should be held in a supportive and mutually
affirming atmosphere. Different interpretations will inevitably
emerge and so there should be some attempt to recognize and
account for the differences. A final report then needs to be
written and the priest might well be the best secretary for the
team, preparing a report for the others to sign. This joint
report will form the basis for the next review.

7   **Communicating results**. The team should determine and agree
   upon the implications of its deliberations and the means by
   which they should be communicated to others. There may,
   after all, be clear indications that changes are necessary in
   aspects of parish life, and it may be necessary to bring specific resolutions to the PCC. Whether or not this is the case, the
   review team should bring a report – a summary rather than
   the full report – to the PCC. The aim here is communication
   and not a second review, and the PCC should be encouraged
   to discuss the conclusions and not the means by which they
   were reached.

8 **Mid-term check.** Roughly halfway to the next review (so after six to nine months) the priest and the review team would helpfully meet to monitor progress towards the objectives and to adjust them if necessary. It can help a priest to have objectives, agreed with the parish, that require special attention. These future plans should be specific, measurable, achievable and compatible.

- 'Specific' means clearly defined such that the desired outcome is clearly understood without the objective being unduly limiting or confining.
- 'Measurable' means that you can see whether or not you are making progress towards the objective.
- 'Achievable' means realistic; an objective may be challenging but it must be possible to reach it within the given time frame.
- 'Compatible' means congruent with other plans and values in the parish and with the agreed distribution of resources.

You may feel, and with some justification, that such a process is a terrifying idea and not one to which you are prepared voluntarily to submit yourself. It requires enormous courage and considerable resilience to go through such a '360 degree' review, and it also calls for a level of maturity from church members which is not, alas, always apparent. It must also be recognized, however, that if priests do not undertake such reviews voluntarily, they may find themselves in the not-too-distant future being forced to undertake them anyway. 'Thou shalt be accountable' is currently the eleventh commandment; the demand for accountability is not going to go away, and recent developments – such as the recommendations in the McClean Report and the Clergy Discipline Measure 2003 – will ensure that it becomes as much a part of church life as it is of other areas of public service. To be at the forefront of the process, to initiate regular reviews and submit oneself to this kind of transparency, will not only serve as the best protection should you unfortunately find yourself faced with a complaint of 'neglect or inefficiency'; it will also demonstrate visionary leadership. By showing that you are prepared to submit yourself to this process of review, without fear and trembling but in a spirit of trust towards those who share in and experience your ministry to the parish, you will encourage a greater sense of maturity and responsibility among those people – as well as a greater degree of understanding of what your work involves and the problems and challenges you face.

But it isn't going to be easy . . .

♦ 7 ♦

Risk management

Two practical 'heresies' seem to have marked church life at various times: to do nothing and leave everything to God, or to do everything and leave nothing to God. As a community marked by faith in God, the local church cannot behave like a straightforward secular business, unwilling to take the sort of risks which are required by obedience to Christ. We trust God to guide and aid us. We take to God in prayer our needs and the needs of the communities we serve. We know there are many instances of the biblical principle 'The Lord will provide' and he does. But we cannot 'do nothing and leave everything to God', for if things go wrong, because we have not discharged our duty of care, it will not be a sufficient defence to say that we left it to God. On the other hand, we cannot expect to remove all risk and we should not want to. Management consultant Dr David Hillson, writing in *Faith in Business Quarterly* (Summer 1999), cited a variety of texts (Genesis 41; Luke 14.28–30; James 4.13–16; Ephesians 5.15; Matthew 10.16) and thought that they suggested 'that faith in God should operate in partnership with a responsible approach to the future' and that 'faith is to be coupled with wisdom, forward planning and preparation wherever possible'. 'The goal,' he said, 'is *maturity with dependency*, recognizing that when we have done our part we can trust God to do the rest.' And he concluded:

> A combined approach becomes possible where the business person also has an active faith. Such a person can not only trust God over uncertainties affecting their personal future, but could also involve God in business decision-making. 'Planning plus prayer' must be a better option than relying solely on human wisdom. This does not absolve believers from the need to manage risk in a professional and structured way, using best-practice

techniques . . . They can however take a different view of residual risk left over after risk management has been undertaken – manage risk proactively as far as possible, then trust God for the rest.

There are nine Rules of Risk Management, according to the advertisement of the RiskMetrics Group <http://www.riskmetrics.com> in *The Economist* (15 May 2004):

1 There is no return without risk.
   Rewards go to those who take risks.
2 Be transparent.
   Risk should be fully understood.
3 Seek experience.
   Risk is measured and managed by people, not mathematical models.
4 Know what you don't know.
   Question the assumptions you make.
5 Communicate.
   Risk should be discussed openly.
6 Diversify.
   Multiple risks will produce more consistent rewards.
7 Show discipline.
   A consistent and rigorous approach will beat a constantly changing strategy.
8 Use common sense.
   It is better to be approximately right, than to be precisely wrong.
9 Return is only half the equation.
   Decisions should be made only by considering the risk and return of the possibilities.

RiskMetrics provides 'risk transparency, expertise, and common sense' for asset managers, banks, corporations, etc. In other words, it deals in financial risk management. Our risks are of a different order but can be approached in a similar common sense way, remembering that we are not seeking to remove risk but to manage it in such a way that we continue to be able to exercise our core ministry *and* that we 'take a different view of residual risk left over after risk management has been undertaken'.

We can identify a number of risk areas:

- the threat to our Christian integrity;
- the threat to reputation, personal and corporate;
- the threat to finances;
- the threat to congregational stability;
- the threat to our ability to carry on with our work.

There is no return without risk

This first RiskMetrics principle is correct. Every time we engage with other people in the name of the Gospel and as ministers of Christ, we take a risk. If we didn't, if we constantly played safe, we would risk nothing for Christ and there would be no reward, here or hereafter.

The priest does not act alone. He or she has a relationship to the bishop marked by both trust and obedience. The structure of the PCC requires the minister to consult with the elected lay members about matters affecting the parish. Professional integrity means that certain courses of action must not be undertaken without the advice and support of other professionals.

Be transparent

This, the second RiskMetrics principle, means that we should not wittingly or unwittingly conceal risk. The risks involved in a course of action need to be set out so that they can be fully understood. So for instance:

- A possible change of position, involving more work or relocation or a change in financial circumstances must be discussed with those involved (parents, spouse, children, etc.).
- The establishment of an open church-based youth club for local young people, who have a bit of a reputation for wild behaviour, needs to be discussed with youth advisers, the PCC, the insurance company, police, and others.

- Agreeing to counsel someone over marital and sexual matters requires prior consultation with a proper supervisor.
- A proposal to convert the church hall for increased community use, involving a partnership with a local authority and considerable financial commitment, requires careful presentation to interested and responsible parties.

Each of these, and many other matters that we could identify, involve a degree of risk. The level of risk needs to be visible and understood, not least because, if in presenting a matter to others we deliberately hide or minimize the risk, we are not acting with integrity. Members of some PCCs will, inevitably, be unfamiliar with risk and its management, and will need more information and greater reassurance before being willing to take a risk, but this is not a reason for (a) not discussing it with them, and (b) avoiding risk whenever possible.

Seek experience

People manage risk all the time. When we ask 'What is the likelihood that we could raise the money for the new roof in time to get the price currently quoted by the contractor?' then we look to those who know something about that sort of fund-raising. We want to know if it is possible and whether, if we sign the contract, we run a risk, possibly an unacceptable risk, of being unable to pay. No mathematical formula will tell you the answer (but most sensible people will tell you never to sign a contract before you have the funding in place). Experience is the key. Parishes too often fail either to seek advice from the diocese, or other bodies, or to find it from within their own communities. 'Seek experience' is a good rule. The minister and churchwardens have a duty to seek the experience that is needed on the PCC and to encourage suitably qualified people to stand for election.

Check assumptions

A necessary part of evaluation is to check assumptions ('know what you don't know'). In the annual presentation to incumbents and treasurers, one diocese began by setting down the assumptions behind the budgetary process and the five-year projection. 'We have assumed,' they said, 'interest rates of n%, income from property of so many thousands rising by n%, reduced expenditure by axing so many posts, savings in the central administration' and so on. Clearly presented, the assumptions could be – and were – questioned. Right or wrong, everyone knew what they were and also knew which were 'guestimates'. If some crucial figure in a budget cannot be determined, then the whole proposal may become too risky.

Communicate

One way to hide what might amount to unacceptable risk is to bury it in a lengthy document. Later, and if it all goes wrong, it will be possible to say that it was in the initial report, in the third foot-note to page 27. (We are not suggesting that you should do this!) The sixth principle is 'Communicate'. We never communicate as well as we think we do and when we are moving people forward in an area of increasing risk, we need to use every means of com-munication available and be sure that all possible questions have been asked and adequately answered. Risk should be discussed openly. We must not be afraid to say 'There is a risk in doing this.' We may go on to say: 'I believe this is an acceptable risk for the following reasons . . .'

Diversify

What might this mean in church terms? Sometimes we are apply-ing our resources in too small a field and we need to broaden our scope. We can do this by looking at what other churches around us provide and seeing if there is a gap in the market. At one church four people turned up every Sunday morning for a said Prayer Book Holy Communion at 9 o'clock. Three other churches in the town offered exactly the same thing at 8 a.m. or 8.30 a.m. An organist was found and the service, though it stayed Prayer Book, had two hymns and the Merbecke Gloria and Creed. Numbers increased to over 20 each Sunday. The needs of a new group of people were addressed. In so far as possible resources allow, a church should offer a more diverse programme.

Show discipline

It is no good, when diversifying, just trying this and trying that, without careful preparation, application and perseverance. Be consistent. Don't keep changing approach. This is true in new ventures and in the discipline of pastoral care.

Once you have worked out what you are offering – house communion, sick visiting, spiritual guidance, marriage preparation, baptism preparation – and you know what resources are needed, offer the programme over not less than a year. So, only a few people bother to come to the baptism class and you have only one person who comes for spiritual guidance, but there is no possibility of building these things up if you keep changing.

Use common sense

It doesn't require some esoteric formula to work a thing out. The basic method for risk management is simple:

(a) What are the risks?
(b) How significant are they?
(c) What can we do about them?
(d) What will we do about them?
(e) How are we getting on?

Risks can be grouped like this:

Christian mission	failure to achieve the basic objectives of the Church
Governance	failure to fill church offices; inability to comply with rules and regulations; breach of trust
Fabric	decay of building; risk of injury; fire risk; risk of theft
Financial	loss of income stream; failure to keep proper records; tax inefficiency; theft

Risks can be identified by brainstorming. Consider the situation if there were no controls – the church is left open and unattended, no one is responsible for switching off lights or heating; collections are counted by anyone who's around; electoral rolls, registers, banns books are left on a shelf in the vestry. Consider the steps you take to remedy this: a rota for locking up, a burglar alarm, sidesmen switching off heating; two people to count the collection; a locked filing cabinet for records. Now consider what happens if any of the systems you have fails. Do you have a back-up? Are you relying too much on one person?

Once risks have been identified, consider the likelihood that something will happen and the impact if it does. In *Churchwardens: A Survival Guide*, we gave an example of a fire risk assessment[24] but we recently came upon an incident that gave it new meaning. In this particular church the great Paschal Candle was lit first thing on Sunday and extinguished after evensong. It was quite a large candle and this year had been rather temperamental: the wick was unsatisfactory and often needed trimming. One Sunday, a week before Pentecost, it was extinguished as usual, but it only *seemed* to go out. There was enough of the candle for it to burn for a week but at some point on Monday a large piece of the candle collapsed and the remaining candle dropped low into the socket generating a great deal of heat. What happened then wasn't clear but on Tuesday morning the church cleaner smelled smoke immediately she opened the door and found the flowers that had been round the candle incinerated, the Perspex drip guard melted and the candle-stick charred. A proper assessment of risk here had to take into consideration compound failure. There was not a high likelihood but the consequences could have been, and fortunately weren't, very serious.

Return is only half the equation

Return for us means people and resources. We put on a programme, lots of people came and they gave lots of money to help us do more. But decisions should be made only when we have considered the risk involved as well as the possible returns. The church bazaar may make a lot of money and attract a lot of people, but perhaps it fills the church building, for weeks, with second-hand books, clothes for sale, bric-a-brac, tea urns, and the like. It no longer looks like a house of prayer but like a flea market. There is a risk of alienating the people you have attracted to use the building for private prayer and quiet days. But on the other hand, the vicar will attract quite a bit of flak if he or she bans the bazaar or insists it move out of the church. The risks needed to be weighed up as well as the returns.

So, every parish minister and every PCC needs to address risk management.

1 Identify risks.
2 Evaluate likelihood and impact.
3 Address the risks; look at how to avoid them, to share the risk (by insurance, for example), or to mitigate it by introducing appropriate systems.
4 Produce a document registering risks.
5 Monitor what you have done.
6 Be alert to new or undiscovered risks and start again.

♦ 8 ♦

Conflict in the parish

Sources of conflict

The peace of the church community can be broken by conflict emanating from a number of sources. One such powerful source is the General Synod. Certain policies adopted by the Synod have a clear effect on parish life and notable recent examples have been liturgical change, the ordination of women and the Anglican-Methodist Covenant. When a PCC is invited to discuss a contentious matter, it will often divide into majority and minority viewpoints. Where the matter is distant or theoretical, division may be of little consequence, but when it concerns life in the parish – Shall we accept an ordained woman here or not? – then the result may be serious conflict and division. The priest may again be caught in a multi-role situation, having personal views on the subject, needing to provide leadership, and needing to care for those who are upset or feel rejected.

Another area of concern is conflict with the local community. The most frequent trigger points are planning matters, the use of the church building, graveyard questions, pastoral reorganization and the possibility of closing the church. In any of these matters the priest will need to be a diplomatist, a communicator and a mediator. Unfortunately, few clergy seem to have these skills (and the clerical author of this work, who thinks he has had more than his fair share of difficulties over artificial flowers, grave sites, and planning consents, does not exclude himself from this criticism) or, if they do have them, they seem to depart as soon as the word 'churchyard' is mentioned. Take this case reported in the journal of the Ecclesiastical Law Society (this and others can be found at <http://www.ecclawsoc.org.uk/cases.html>):

The team rector and churchwardens sought a faculty to remove 'all unauthorized materials, including ornamental edgings, chippings and freestanding items, from graves in the churchyard'. There was considerable opposition from families who had introduced such items. The chancellor found that the unlawful additions to the graves were put in position without permission and, as a matter of pure law, were a trespass. They contravened the chancellor's guidelines and made maintenance more difficult. Failure to prevent or remove such additions did not amount to a waiver of the rules. However, he found that interference with the additions (which had been tolerated for a number of years) would be deeply resented by those who used such memorials to help in their grief. The chancellor stated that the materials in question may remain until further order and gave the petitioners leave to reapply for the removal of additions to such graves as were not maintained in good order and for removal of such additions as would impede the transfer of the maintenance of the churchyard to the local authority in due course. The chancellor directed that no further such unlawful additions were to be made and that the rector, churchwardens and PCC were to take steps to clarify the need to obtain permission to erect a memorial.

This is not in any way an unusual case. Unfortunately the repercussions within the local community can go on for years.

The largest generator of conflict is, however, internal – clashes between people and groups within the church community that purport to be concerned with policies and theologies but are usually much more about people, their likes, their dislikes, and their sometimes bitter enmities.

The 'dust ball' phenomenon

Some unexpected incident in the life of the parish may trigger the 'dust ball' phenomenon. Itself of little consequence, this incident becomes a focus, rolling along and gathering up complaints of various sorts. As it rolls it grows, and must in consequence be dealt with early on, if at all possible. 'People are saying' is a related phenomenon: churchwardens and other church officers take the minister on one side with something they wish to talk about and begin 'People are saying . . .'. 'Which people?' one old-school training incumbent would always reply, stressing that those with real concerns would always be willing to be named, but the minister has to be fairly thick-skinned to adopt such an approach. Church-wardens often see themselves, and rightly, to a degree, as those who must listen to the complaints and concerns of the parish and congregation and communicate them to the minister but possibly also to the archdeacon and bishop. The minister wonders who the unnamed people are, can sometimes guess, and could usually give a context for the complaint. When there is a genuine complaint of some sort, churchwardens must encourage the use of the parish complaints procedure,[25] but 'people are saying' rarely gives rise to a specific complaint. It is made up of a number of things. People in church can be aggrieved for all sorts of reasons: they do not like the minister or the changes introduced or new people or different hymns or a thousand and one other things. We can, however, identify certain types of aggrieved people that occur fairly frequently. The process begins with the arrival of a new minister but may not become a real difficulty for years:

1 The disempowered: people who previously wielded a great deal of power in a parish may find their offices given to others and their links to the vicarage severed by a new minister who gathers other friends and advisers; they resent it.

2 The disappointed: these had high hopes that the new minister would support their cause whatever it was and be pro- or anti- the ordination of women, new liturgies, family services, the Book of Common Prayer, the Authorized Version, youth work, the old folks' luncheon club, artificial flowers in the churchyard, etc., etc. When the minister, whom they at first welcomed enthusiastically, follows a path they don't agree with, they turn into opponents.

3 The defeated: attempting to persuade the PCC to follow or oppose a certain course of action, these people are defeated by those they consider to be 'the minister's clique'. After one or two defeats, they criticize everything the minister proposes and constantly seek to inflict a defeat on him or her themselves.

4   The mad: churches attract more than their fair share of mad
    people whose behaviour, if not clinically insane, is at the least
    irrational, unpredictable and sometimes inappropriate. Such
    people are easily gathered into a 'dust ball'.

Once there is a focus for complaint, the next stage is often a
campaign of destabilization. One well-tried approach is that of the
unsubtle hint backed up by innuendo and gossip: key people are
contacted with the suggestion of trouble to come – congregational
concern, a formal complaint, legal action, a newspaper story. The
person against whom this campaign is directed will find that the
phone constantly rings as the bishop, the archdeacon, the chairman
of the parish council or whoever else seeks information. The
conversation begins with reference to a letter, a telephone call or a
conversation – 'Someone said to me the other day . . .'. This back-
ground rumbling creates a sense of unease and anxiety – and it
is intended to do so; like a series of small bush fires, it is much
harder to deal with than a blaze concentrated in one place. Those
responsible for such action do not want to be named and are
unable to produce any evidence for what they say, but they can
cause a great deal of concern. They want to destabilize the situation
and to bring about precipitate action. For this reason it is important to write a summary of the actual issues at stake, of what has
actually given rise to discontent, even if it is initially only for your
own use. Without such a focus these small things can seem to be
very much larger than they really are. The power people have is
chiefly the power we give them, the power to upset us.
    If there is a real story and it is given to the press (see the next
section) the process of destabilization will continue. In one incident, with a story carefully placed in the tabloid press, one of those
responsible left a series of voicemail messages urging that the paper
should be bought the next day. The same person rang a church-
warden the next day to deplore the damage done to the church,
to report on the concern of highly placed people, and to advise
mediation. This is an example of 'setting fire to the house in order
to help put it out'. He then rang a local councillor, a friend of the
incumbent, to report that there had been uproar at the Sunday
services because of the newspaper article. This was not true but
was again a way to fan the flames.

Managing conflict

Training, mediation and consultancy in conflict management are available from various organizations, such as, for instance, the Bridge Builders programme of the London Mennonite Centre (see Resources section). Useful information can also be found at askNCVO <http://www.ncvo-vol.org.uk/asp/search/main.aspx>, the NCVO's online best practice resource. The NCVO points out that disputes can prove costly in terms of time, uncertainty of outcome, damaging publicity, relationships and morale, stress and in some cases legal fees, and that mediation is a proven method of dispute resolution. In mediation the parties themselves work out a mutually acceptable solution, with the help of a neutral mediator. The stages involved in mediation are:

- relevant information is shared by each party and mediator, before the mediation;
- the parties meet both in confidential discussions with the mediator and face to face with each other as appropriate;
- the parties may be accompanied by legal or other representatives agreed between the parties beforehand;
- if the mediation is successful, a written agreement is drawn up immediately and its implementation planned;
- the mediator facilitates the process but the parties are responsible for the outcome.

The NCVO provides mediation jointly with the Centre for Effective Dispute Resolution (CEDR) in a scheme administered by CEDR Solve, CEDR's dispute resolution and prevention service. Most mediations are settled in a day; the costs are set on a sliding scale depending on the financial size of the charitable organization involved. The scheme does extend to churches.

In dealing with any kind of conflict it is useful to be aware of one's own 'conflict style' – that is, the collection of attitudes, beliefs and behaviours that constitute the way you approach conflict. By way of an introduction to conflict styles, you could do worse than go to <http://www.hrpress-diversity.com/rc2k/constylequest.html> and fill out the conflict style questionnaire to determine (approximately) your profile. There are eight possible styles listed:

1 cautious (delays confrontation, avoids conflict);
2 seeking (sees potential conflict in many situations);
3 strong (values winning conflicts, takes a firm position);
4 peaceful (values peace, hesitates to express needs);
5 calm (controls emotions, remains calm in heated situations);
6 feeling (uses strong emotional tone to make convincing arguments);
7 compromising (seeks a quick middle ground position, exchanges concessions);
8 solution-focused (views conflicts as problems to be solved, believes it is important to satisfy the needs and goals of both parties).

While we are not suggesting that knowing your conflict style will help you to avoid conflict, having some understanding of how your own and other people's styles interact may help you to find new ways of dealing with it, and to determine whether your style – in conjunction with those of the other people involved – may be making the situation worse. If you realize that your particular style is likely to infuriate a group of people, for instance, you might ask someone with a different style to put your case for you. Or you may discover that by modifying your style you can reduce the temperature of the conflict and find that the substance is not so very significant after all.

Sometimes, however, conflicts go too far to be solved by mediation or questions of style.

♦ 9 ♦

'Dear Bishop, I wish to complain . . .'

Complaints

The Church of England does not have a complaints procedure, and it has further confused matters, in the new Clergy Discipline Measure, by using a letter of complaint as the trigger for disciplinary proceedings. Clearly that sort of letter of complaint is of rather a particular kind. There is, however, a tendency to complain nowadays and to do so directly to the diocesan bishop, or even to the archbishop. People who complain directly to the clergy are likely to copy the letter to bishop and archdeacon. As there are no published complaint procedures on diocesan websites we have no firm evidence for the handling of complaints made to the bishops but most dioceses follow a procedure like this:

The bishop receives a letter of complaint about a matter that does not amount prima facie to serious misconduct; he acknowledges it and says that he is passing it to the archdeacon for investigation. The archdeacon responds to the complainant, says that he or she will investigate and copies the letter to the bishop and to the priest involved. The archdeacon also asks the priest to investigate the matter and report back to the archdeacon or perhaps to write directly to the complainant with an explanation and copy it to the archdeacon. The priest does so and, if it is not a serious or complicated matter, that may be the end of it, though a few more letters may go backwards and forwards, being copied to everyone. The bishop or, more likely, the archdeacon may well apologize to the complainant *before* investigating the matter, hence conveying the impression that the priest is in the wrong. (Note to archdeacons: do not apologize for your clergy; they can do it themselves if they need to.) If you have a parish complaints procedure and it is obviously a complaint that can be dealt with within the parish, the archdeacon may be willing for it to be handled in that way, with a copy of the report going to the archdeacon's office.

Let us suppose that the complaint is a more serious one concerning some sort of conduct unbecoming a clerk in Holy Orders. Let us say that you are accused of being drunk while conducting a funeral service – not after the event but before and during it, evidenced by slurred speech, inability to walk straight, etc. – and that the letter of complaint has come from the funeral director with supporting letters from the family. This amounts to a valid and documented complaint. The bishop is again likely, after consulting the diocesan registrar, to ask the archdeacon to investigate. He or she will, therefore, seek any further information from the complainant, including possibly asking what outcome the complainant is seeking. This may be an important question. The complainant may be doing little more than letting off steam, or else feeling that the matter should be brought to the attention of the diocese, or may be looking for an apology, rather than seeking the imposition of punishment. The archdeacon then invites your comments. You confess that you had had a boozy lunch with the churchwardens, forgetting the funeral, and that yes, you were drunk. Or perhaps you explain that you stood in at the last moment for another priest who was involved in a car accident; you were literally summoned from the pub on your day off because no other priest was available. Or you protest that you were not drunk at all but the medication for your diabetes sometimes produces a side effect of making you appear to be drunk. Or you deny it emphatically and say the complainant is lying and all because you would not let them have 'O valiant hearts'. Or you admit that recently the stress of ministry has all become too much for you and you fear that you have a drink problem. Five scenarios: each of which will require a different response from archdeacon and bishop. Three of them will not lead to a formal hearing; one of them might; the other one almost certainly will.

At present the diocesan bishop has very few options open to him and in consequence will always seek a pastoral solution and your help in achieving it, unless it is clear to him that there is a prima facie case of pretty serious misconduct. The range of actions open to him will change when the Clergy Discipline Measure comes into effect.

Disciplinary procedures: how they work

The Ecclesiastical Jurisdiction Measure 1963 repealed all the previous disciplinary acts and measures. Offences against the laws ecclesiastical are divided by this measure into two: those that involve matters of doctrine, ritual or ceremonial, and other offences. The latter category – the only one that concerns us here – includes, but is not limited to, conduct unbecoming the office and work of a clerk in holy orders and serious, persistent or continuous neglect of duty – familiar offences already found in the Incumbents (Discipline) Measure 1947. This Measure allowed for proceedings to be instituted against 'the incumbent of any benefice in respect of conduct unbecoming the character of a clerk in Holy Orders or of serious, persistent or continuous neglect of duty' (s. 2). Halsbury's *Ecclesiastical Law* states that the expression 'offences against the laws ecclesiastical' includes 'Statutory offences (namely offences under relevant Acts of Parliament and under Measures of the Church Assembly or General Synod), offences under the common law of the realm in matters ecclesiastical, and breaches of post-Reformation canons'.

The two areas that should particularly concern us are conduct unbecoming and neglect of duty. Halsbury states that 'There is no statutory definition of unbecoming conduct for this purpose, but it would appear to cover any such acts, conducts or habits as would contravene the provisions of the canons as to the manner of life of the clergy.'

The list given by Halsbury of acts that have been held to be offences includes drunkenness, frequenting alehouses and tippling (this in 1700!), incontinence (in the sense of unchastity), habitual swearing and ribaldry, irreverent language in the pulpit, writing a rude letter to a parishioner or an obscene letter to an unmarried woman, the solicitation of chastity, the collection of alms on false pretences, the forgery of orders and cruelty to a servant. 'Neglect of duty' also has a fairly open definition, being interpreted as 'the failure without due cause to perform an ecclesiastical duty', and it therefore applies primarily but not exclusively to those, such as incumbents, whose duties are laid down by law.

Proceedings under the 1963 Measure are instituted – the Measure is still in force at the time of writing – by way of a complaint laid before the registrar of the diocese in which the priest or deacon held or holds preferment or in which he resided or resides at the date of the alleged offence or of the complaint. A complaint may only be validly made by certain complainants: in the case of an incumbent

(a) by an authorized complainant (i.e. one authorized by the bishop to deal with that particular complaint – this may, for instance, be the archdeacon);
(b) by six or more persons of full age whose names are on the electoral roll of the parish.

Proceedings not involving doctrine are tried by the consistory court and the priest or deacon may be suspended while proceedings are pending.

It is a basic principle of this Measure that pastoral problems should be dealt with without recourse to litigation. The bishop initially affords the accused and the complainant the opportunity of a private interview after which he may

(a) decide that no further action shall be taken, or
(b) refer the complaint for an inquiry.

As in the 1947 Measure, the accused may admit the offence of which he is accused and the bishop may, after consulting the complainant, pronounce censure, and no further steps are then taken in the matter. If the matter proceeds to inquiry, this is carried out by an examiner selected by ballot from a panel appointed by the diocesan synod. The parties may be assisted or represented at any inquiry before an examiner. Evidence is given by affidavit but oral evidence may also be given under oath. After complainant and accused have lodged affidavits and given notice of those who will be called as witnesses, the examiner decides whether there is a case to answer. If the decision is that there is no case to answer, then no further steps must be taken. If there is a case to answer the examiner must specify the offence and a person must be nominated to promote the complaint.

Within 28 days of being nominated, the promoter must lodge with the registrar articles (i.e. a statement) containing the offence or offences specified by an examiner and a copy must be served on the accused. Within 14 days the accused may lodge an answer and serve a copy on the complainant. An answer must admit or deny each offence, and may admit or deny, or give the accused's account or explanation of, the matters alleged in the articles to constitute each offence. Each offence must be charged separately and the articles must allege all facts required to constitute the offence.

The bishop can also suspend you from work. This is known as 'inhibition *pendente lite*'. The bishop can serve a notice on a priest inhibiting him or her from performing any services within his diocese from a specified date until the proceedings are concluded if it appears to him that it is desirable in the interests of the church that he should do so. Your solicitor can and should argue the case for you not to be inhibited, as suspension immediately gives rise to gossip and perhaps to media interest, and you are not in a position to defend yourself by making any sort of statement at this time. An incumbent, if inhibited, may nominate a fit person to perform the services, who is then licensed by the bishop.

The trial takes place within 28 days of the lodging of the articles and follows the same basic procedures as a Crown Court in a criminal case. The diocesan chancellor presides, sitting with four assessors – two priests, two lay – chosen by ballot from the diocesan panels. The assessors function as the jury. If the accused admits the offence, the matter is considered proven and evidence can be dispensed with. Otherwise, evidence is given orally in open court. The court has the same power, in relation to the calling, attendance and examination of witnesses and the production and inspection of documents, as does the High Court. If the accused is found guilty, the court decides the censure, which is then written down and pronounced in open court.

There are various appeal processes, including appeal, by the complainant or the accused, against the original decision of the registrar; appeal to a higher court – the Court of Arches or the Chancery Court of York – on questions of law or matters of fact is permitted. The accused may also appeal against the decision of the court, within 28 days, stating the grounds for the appeal, and the appeal is heard by all the judges of the higher court.

The censures available to the court under the 1963 Measure are:

1   Deprivation – removal from any preferment, and disqualification from holding future preferment; deprivation may be followed by deposition from holy orders.
2   Inhibition – disqualification from exercising priestly functions for a specified time.
3   Suspension – 'disqualification of a person for a specified time from exercising or performing without the bishop's leave any right or duty of or incidental to his preferment or from residing in the house of residence of his preferment or within such distance of it as is specified in the censure' (Halsbury, para. 1378). Various conditions, e.g. not interfering in the running of the parish, are attached to both inhibition and suspension.
4   Monition – an order to do or refrain from doing a specified act.
5   Rebuke.

The point is made in Halsbury that

in determining the appropriate censure, the court acts in a judicial, not a pastoral, capacity, and the paramount consideration is the gravity of the offence and not the well-being of the parish as a whole, although if an offence merits a particular censure the judge, in deciding whether to pronounce it, may take into consideration all relevant considerations including the interests of the parish. (para 1372)

The Incumbents (Vacation of Benefices) Measure 1977

The Incumbents (Vacation of Benefices) Measure 1977 makes provision (to quote its long title) 'for the vacation of the benefice, where there has been a serious breakdown of the pastoral relationship or where an incumbent is unable by reason of age or infirmity to discharge adequately the duties attaching to his benefice'. It has been repealed and amended in part by subsequent measures, most notably by the Incumbents (Vacation of Benefices) (Amendment) Measure 1993. In effect the 1977 Measure extended the powers granted by the Ecclesiastical Jurisdiction Measure 1963.

The term 'breakdown' in the 1977 Measure means, and is confined to, the breakdown of the pastoral relationship between the incumbent and his or her parishioners, but the 1993 Measure defined it more carefully:

> In this Measure any reference to a serious breakdown of the pastoral relationship between an incumbent and the parishioners shall be construed as a reference to a situation where the relationship between an incumbent and the parishioners of the parish in question is such as to impede the promotion in the parish of the whole mission of the Church of England, pastoral, evangelistic, social and ecumenical (s. 10).

In March 1999 the Lords of the Judicial Committee of the Privy Council delivered a judgment in the case of the Reverend Ashley Cheesman and others v. The Church Commissioners.[26] The case, which ultimately concerned the application of the Pastoral Measure 1983, also involved actions taken under the Ecclesiastical Jurisdiction Measure 1963 and the Incumbents (Vacation of Benefices) Measure 1977. The Lords delivered a majority judgment rejecting the appeal, with Lord Lloyd of Berwick giving a dissenting judgment that would have upheld the appeal. The full judgment, including Lord Lloyd's dissenting judgment, can be found at <http://www.privy-council.org.uk/output/page170.asp>.

The origins of the case were summarized by Lord Lloyd:

> The Reverend Ashley Cheesman became incumbent in February 1988. It appears that he had been one of three applicants for the benefice. The other two had dropped out at the last moment. Mr. Cheesman had previously been curate at an inner city parish in Birkenhead. It soon became apparent that Mr. Cheesman's ministry was not to everybody's liking. Within eight months the churchwarden of St. Peter's Gaulby had resigned, because of Mr. Cheesman's 'excessively evangelistic approach in the pulpit', and his perceived failure to meet the pastoral needs of his parishioners.
>
> Then came the event which has accentuated discord within the parish. On 30th January 1989 Mr. Cheesman was charged with wilfully and indecently exposing himself in a public lavatory in Abbey Park, Leicester. On 26th September 1989 he was convicted, having given no evidence in his own defence. He was duly

suspended from his duties under section 77 of the Ecclesiastical Jurisdiction Measure 1963. However on 19th October 1990 Mr. Cheesman's conviction was quashed on the ground that the prosecution had failed to prove an essential element in the offence, namely, annoyance to the public. The only witnesses present in the public lavatory were two police officers. Upon his conviction being quashed, his suspension lapsed. But a complaint was made the same day under section 14 of the Ecclesiastical Jurisdiction Measure by the Archdeacon of Leicester, charging Mr. Cheesman with the ecclesiastical offence of conduct unbecoming the office and work of a clerk in Holy Orders, and a fresh suspension was issued the same day by the acting Bishop of Leicester.

Meanwhile a number of Mr. Cheesman's parishioners had written to the Bishop requesting an inquiry under section 1 of the Incumbents (Vacation of Benefices) Measure 1977 on the ground that there had been a serious breakdown of the pastoral relationship between Mr. Cheesman and his parishioners. The acting Bishop appointed the Archdeacon of Loughborough to carry out an investigation under section 3 of the Measure.

The Archdeacon had meetings with the church wardens on 12th and 20th November 1990, and with representatives of the seven villages on 22nd and 27th November. On 11th December he had a meeting with Mr. Cheesman. Two days later he wrote to the acting Bishop to state his preliminary findings. These were that: '. . . the support for the incumbent shown by a few parishioners is far outweighed by the vast majority view that serious breakdown over a substantial period not only exists, but is irretrievable.'

On 24th December 1990 he wrote again: 'It is not for me . . . to anticipate the findings of an official inquiry. My task . . . is to satisfy myself that in terms of Part I of the Measure, there is sufficient evidence to warrant an inquiry into the pastoral situation in the benefice. Perhaps the strongest reason leading me to believe that there is, is the realisation that there is no common ground between the incumbent and most of his parishioners as to whether there is a breakdown or not. When very many believe there is such a breakdown, and give chapter and verse to support their assertion, and the incumbent believes that all is well except for the activities of a very small minority of malicious ill-wishers, it is clearly time for an impartial panel to examine the evidence and judge accordingly.'

It will suffice here to say that an inquiry followed but was beset by problems from the outset – one tribunal member retired on grounds of ill health, one became a bishop, another had a heart attack. The total bill for the inquiry was already £100,000 after a year with little hope of progress. The Bishop of Leicester called a halt and, as Mr Cheesman was unwilling to move to another appointment, proposed a Pastoral Scheme transferring most of his parish to another benefice.

The majority judgment includes this description of procedures under the 1977 Measure:

> The 1977 Measure is based on considerations of incompetence or inadequacy on the part of the incumbent evidenced by a serious breakdown of pastoral relations between the incumbent and the laity in a benefice. The inquiry required is directed not only to whether there has in fact been such a breakdown but also to whether it is attributable to deficiencies on the part of the incumbent. The breakdown in relations may, for example, have been attributable to parishioners not the incumbent. A declaration of the vacation of the benefice, i.e. the total depriva- tion of the incumbent of his freehold, can only be justified if both these criteria have been satisfied. It is this structure which makes the implementation of the 1977 procedures so cumbersome and uncertain in outcome. The remedy of vacation of benefice necessarily involves criticism of the incumbent; the investigation of the seriousness of the breakdown and the responsibility for it are inevitably involved.

Lord Lloyd made further observations on the relation between and application of the Measures in this case as follows:

> The powers exercisable under the Ecclesiastical Jurisdiction Measure go back a very long way. They enable an incumbent to be deprived of his freehold benefice where he has been found guilty of unbecoming conduct, or serious neglect of duty. But

these powers, extensive though they are, were not designed to deal with serious pastoral breakdown. Nor, of course, did they cover the case of an incumbent who is simply too old or too infirm to discharge his duties. One can see therefore that there was a need for a Measure to cover these eventualities. One can see also that in the case of pastoral breakdown there was a need for some sort of impartial inquiry. For it is not to be assumed that pastoral breakdown will always be due to the conduct of the incumbent. It may equally be due to the conduct of his parishioners. Since one consequence of an inquiry might be a declaration of avoidance depriving the incumbent of his freehold benefice, the incumbent was clearly entitled to a fair hearing.

The Measure which was designed to meet these diverse objectives had a long gestation period. There may be many who share the Bishop's view that the Incumbents (Vacation of Benefices) Measure is 'deeply flawed'. Obviously reconciliation between the incumbent and his parishioners should be the preferred solution. This is now made clear by section 1A(1A) of the amended Measure, and by the new Code of Practice issued under the amended section 1.

Another defect is that the procedure is much too cumbersome and expensive. There is room for the sort of simplification which Lord Woolf's reforms are designed to bring about in civil proceedings. But that said, there was undoubtedly a gap which needed to be filled. In the case of irreconcilable breakdown of the pastoral relationship, the procedure designed by the General Synod, and approved by Parliament, is that set out in the Measure. Nowhere in the discussions which preceded the passing of the Measure, or in the Code of Practice issued by the House of Bishops, is it suggested that pastoral breakdown, where it exists within a parish, can be resolved by the simple process of splitting the parish in two under the Pastoral Measure of 1983. On the contrary it is clear from paragraph 3 of the Code of Practice that the three Measures, that is to say the Ecclesiastical Jurisdiction Measure 1963, the Incumbents (Vacation of Benefices) Measure 1977 and the Pastoral Measure 1983 are all different in their origin and distinct in their purposes. They are not interchangeable. The Incumbents (Vacation of Benefices) Measure provides a complete statutory code in the case of pastoral breakdown.

The safeguards which it provides are not to be bypassed. Such safeguards include the incumbent's right to opt for a provincial tribunal. The Bishop has made clear his view that there has been a serious pastoral breakdown in the parish. Mr. Cheesman disagrees. His case is that the opposition to his Ministry is confined to a small but vociferous group in Burton Overy and Carlton Curlieu. Parliament has provided a procedure which is specifically designed to resolve that issue. On the face of it the alleged pastoral breakdown in Gaulby falls fairly and squarely within the provisions of the Incumbents (Vacation of Benefices) Measure.

Perhaps unsurprisingly, the Cheesman case is the last reported application of the 1977 Measure. Its application, as Lord Lloyd said, is cumbersome and expensive, though the 1993 amendments did address some of the problems. The Measure remains on the statute book as a last resort when it has not been possible to remove the causes of estrangement between the incumbent and the parishioners and to promote better relations between them.

Secular proceedings and Church discipline

If a priest is found guilty of certain acts in criminal or civil proceedings, certain ecclesiastical consequences may follow. The acts fall into two broad categories: offences and matrimonial matters. If a priest is convicted of any offence and a sentence of imprisonment is passed, whether suspended or not, the priest is liable to deprivation. If a priest is divorced by his or her spouse, and the grounds for divorce are adultery, unreasonable behaviour or desertion, the priest is liable to deprivation. This is also the case if a priest is found, in a matrimonial case, to have committed adultery, or has certain types of order made against him (affiliation, matrimonial, or an order on the ground of wilful neglect of wife or child).

On receiving a court certificate, the bishop must refer the case to the archbishop, with his own recommendation and with a copy of any written representations made by the priest. Within two months the archbishop must make a declaration of deprivation or disqualification unless he determines, on the basis of the representations made, that he should not do so. If deprived, the priest is again liable to be deposed from holy orders.

Deposition and its effects

Deposition from holy orders has the same effect as if the priest had executed a deed, under the Clerical Disabilities Act 1870, relinquishing all the rights and privileges of office. Halsbury describes its effect in this way:

> the clergyman who executed it becomes incapable of officiating or acting as a minister of the Church of England and of holding any preferment in it, and ceases to enjoy the rights, privileges and exemptions attached to the office of such a minister, and every licence, office and place held by him, which must by law be held by a minister of the Church of England becomes ipso facto void. The clergyman also becomes discharged and free from all disabilities, disqualifications and restraints to which he would otherwise have been subject as a person admitted to the office of minister in the Church of England, and from all jurisdiction, penalties, censures and proceedings to which he would or might otherwise have been amenable or liable in consequence of his having been so admitted, or of anything done or omitted by him after such admission. (para. 687)

As the church considers priesthood to be indelible, it is possible for a person who has relinquished his or her orders or who has been deposed from them to be restored to them, without any re-ordination, but under very strict conditions.

The Clergy Discipline Measure 2003

(The following description of the Measure is based on the report made by the General Synod's Legislative Committee to the Ecclesiastical Committee of Parliament.)

The working party that produced the Measure was appointed by the General Synod in November 1992 to review the law relating to the discipline of the clergy and the ecclesiastical courts. The Ecclesiastical Jurisdiction Measure 1963 (as noted previously) divided clergy discipline into two: cases concerning morality, unbecoming conduct and neglect of duty on the one hand, and those concerned with doctrine, ritual and ceremonial on the other. For the former, the court of first instance was the Consistory Court;

for the latter, it was the new Court of Ecclesiastical Causes Reserved. Since 1963 only a few disciplinary cases have reached the Consistory Court and no disciplinary cases have been taken to the Court of Ecclesiastical Causes Reserved. The working party came to the conclusion that the system's inflexibility and cost led to the increasing unwillingness of bishops to use the 1963 Measure. The working party proposed new disciplinary structures, reaffirmed the role of the bishop in clergy discipline, and proposed that the Archbishops' Caution List should become the official depository of decisions made under due process. The new Measure would apply to all in Holy Orders, whether freehold, licensed, stipendiary or not, active or retired, and agreed that the following should be regarded as disciplinary offences:

1 wilful disobedience to or breach of the laws ecclesiastical;
2 neglect, culpable carelessness or gross inefficiency in the performance of the duties of office;
3 conduct inappropriate or unbecoming to the office;
4 teaching, preaching, publishing or professing doctrine or belief incompatible with that of the Church of England.

The report *Under Authority: Report on Clergy Discipline* was submitted to the Synod in November 1996. The proposals were approved subject to two amendments. The first provided that cases involving doctrine, ritual and ceremonial should remain under the 1963 Measure and the second retained the existing provisions whereby disciplinary proceedings could not be instituted in respect of political opinions or activities. A draft measure was submitted to the Synod in 1999, received general approval, and was referred to a revision committee. The Measure was then revised in full Synod in February and July 2000. The Final Drafting and Final Approval stages were taken in November 2000 and it was expected to receive parliamentary approval in 2001. Because the Churchwardens Measure was held up, it didn't actually reach the Ecclesiastical Committee until 2003 and it was 'deemed expedient'. It cannot come into operation, however, until the Clergy Discipline Commission established by the Measure to oversee its workings has produced a Code of Practice, which must also be agreed by the General Synod. The Rule Committee also needs to produce the

Rules for the operation of the tribunals. The provisions of the Measure concerning clergy discipline are not therefore expected to come into force until at least January 2006. The full text can be found at <http://www.legislation.hmso.gov.uk/measures/20030003. htm>.

In brief, the Measure will introduce a procedure in the way detailed here. The procedure will be initiated by a complaint being made to the bishop. Only written and identifiable complaints will be permitted and anonymous complaints will be disregarded.

There will then be a *sieve procedure* with the diocesan registrar advising the bishop on three matters:

- Under the Measure, has the complainant the right to complain?
- If the complaint is found to be valid, would the complaint be a disciplinary matter?
- What quality of evidence is being offered in support of the complaint?

A complaint can be made by:

1 a person nominated by the parochial church council of any parish which has a proper interest in making the complaint, if not less than two-thirds of the lay members of the council are present at a duly convened meeting of the council and not less than two-thirds of the lay members present and voting pass a resolution to the effect that the proceedings be insti- tuted; or
2 a churchwarden of any such parish; or
3 any other person who has a proper interest in making the complaint. (s. 10 (1) (a))

It may allege any of the following acts or omissions:

1 doing any act in contravention of the laws ecclesiastical;
2 failing to do any act required by the laws ecclesiastical;
3 neglect or inefficiency in the performance of the duties of his office;
4 conduct unbecoming or inappropriate to the office and work of a clerk in Holy Orders. (s. 8 (1))

There is a time limitation (with some exceptions):

> No disciplinary proceedings under this Measure shall be insti-
> tuted unless the misconduct in question, or the last instance of it
> in the case of a series of acts or omissions, occurred within the
> period of one year ending with the date on which proceedings
> are instituted. (s. 9)

On the basis of the Registrar's advice, the bishop *determines*
whether or not it is a disciplinary matter. He also determines if the
complaint is frivolous, malicious or vexatious – in which case it is
rejected. If the complaint is not disciplinary, it proceeds no further.
If it is disciplinary the bishop decides which of the five *procedures*
is appropriate:

1 no further action;
2 left on the record;
3 conciliation;
4 penalty with consent;
5 tribunal.

The Measure only gives a broad outline of these and it does not
indicate, for example, when the accused will be informed of the
nature of the complaint and given an opportunity to respond to it.
We must wait for the appearance of the Code of Practice and the
Rules. The draft Code of Practice appended to the draft measure
was for illustrative purposes only but it did indicate that the
procedures covered both professional and personal conduct.
Professional conduct, as defined by the draft Code, includes:

1 Public worship and occasional offices conducted according
   to the authorized forms and in a seemly, reverent and pastoral
   manner.
2 Preaching and teaching of the Gospel and Christian faith in
   order to bring people to, and build them up in, Christian
   discipleship.
3 Pastoral care of people, not least of those in vulnerable situations who can easily be abused unless proper provision is
   made available.

4   Good administration, which is an aspect of pastoral care, and is essential to the proper running of parishes and chaplaincies.
5   Leadership in the Church to guard and shape its mission. This will involve collaboration with others, due respect for those in authority, and partnership in appropriate levels of synodical government.

The Measure has six **penalties** that may be imposed that vary slightly from those in the 1963 Measure:

1   prohibition for life, that is to say prohibition without limit of time from exercising any of the functions of his Orders;
2   limited prohibition, that is to say prohibition for a specific time from exercising any of the functions of his Orders;
3   removal from office, that is to say, removal from any preferment which he then holds;
4   in the case of a minister licensed to serve in a diocese by the bishop thereof, revocation of the licence;
5   injunction, that is to say, an order to do or to refrain from doing a specified act;
6   rebuke.

'Prohibition for life' has replaced deprivation followed by deposition.
   The 2003 Measure includes ecclesiastical penalties that follow on conviction in the secular courts and imprisonment, and on being divorced with a finding of adultery, unreasonable behaviour or desertion. It also adds a duty to disclose criminal convictions and arrests, an absolute divorce decree or an order for judicial separation. Failure to disclose them would be an ecclesiastical offence.

What should you do if a formal complaint is made against you by an individual or group of individuals?

The bishop receives a complaint against you making a series of allegations and clearly intended to be a formal complaint within the meaning of the Measure. If it is not clear from your first contact with the bishop or archdeacon how the complaint against you is going to be handled, then ask before you make any response to the complaint. As a general rule, you should not give an answer to a complaint in writing at this stage as this will not constitute a legally privileged communication. If the bishop or archdeacon asks to see you, ask what sort of interview it will be, i.e. is it an investigative interview? You have the right to be accompanied to the interview by a union representative (if you have joined Amicus), by a friend, or by your solicitor. You should also check – depending on the nature of the complaint – whether you are covered by the church insurance policy for legal representation. If you have an ordinary solicitor, he or she is probably not familiar with ecclesiastical law. You cannot ask the diocesan registrar for advice at this point, because he is one of your bishop's officers. You can ask the registrar of another diocese but you will, of course, have to pay his or her fees. Nevertheless, it is worth consulting someone familiar with the ecclesiastical law and the disciplinary procedures. The contact details of diocesan registrars can be found in the *Church of England Year Book*. You should, without giving details, tell your churchwardens (unless they are party to it) that a complaint has been made against you. The less you say at this stage the better.

If you admit the offence, then, as stated above, the bishop can pronounce censure and that is an end of it. If you deny the alleged offence, the bishop must offer both you and the complainant the opportunity of a private interview. Again, you have the right to be accompanied and you should be. The bishop may decide that no further action should be taken, and otherwise refers the matter for inquiry, as set out above. He can also suspend you from work. Your solicitor can and should argue the case for you not to be suspended, as suspension immediately gives rise to gossip and perhaps to media interest, and you are not in a position to defend yourself by making any sort of statement at this time. The procedure is then that set out above, until the Clergy Discipline Measure comes into force.

It cannot be stressed too strongly that you should *not* turn to the bishop, archdeacon, rural or area dean, diocesan registrar, or any other member of the diocesan hierarchy for advice on a matter that could lead to disciplinary proceedings. Any one of them can be party to the disciplinary action taken against you. To reinforce this it is only necessary to refer to the canons. Canon C 22 (4) 'Of archdeacons' states:

> Every archdeacon shall within his archdeaconry carry out his duties under the bishop and shall assist the bishop in his pastoral care and office, and particularly he shall see that all such as hold any ecclesiastical office within the same perform their duties with diligence, and *shall bring to the bishop's attention what calls for correction or merits praise.* [Our emphasis]

Canon C 23 (1) 'Of rural deans' states:

> Every rural dean *shall report to the bishop any matter in any parish within the deanery which it may be necessary or useful for the bishop to know,* particularly any case of serious illness or other form of distress amongst the clergy . . . [Our emphasis]

One priest, anxious about an allegation made about him that might appear in the press, went to talk to his archdeacon. The archdeacon told him that, in the circumstances that he had outlined, he ought to resign; if he didn't, the archdeacon would initiate a complaint and suspend him. He was more or less told to go quietly and there would be no further trouble. With no information about his rights, he resigned. This was quite simply abuse of power and a violation of human rights. The hierarchy are, however, caught in a double bind: they cannot function as colleagues, counsellors, pastors, as well as prosecutors and judges. If you need advice, you must seek it elsewhere.

♦ 10 ♦

Crisis management

What constitutes a crisis?

So far we have been concerned with preventing things going wrong, with dealing with events as they start to slip out of control, and with people who deliberately, wilfully cause trouble within the parish and for the priest. Now we come to crisis management. Many things give rise to crises of different levels of intensity:

- disaster in the form of preventable fire, serious accident or terrorism;
- public resignation of church officers in protest against the priest;
- suicide related to some church event or person;
- death of a church member by accident, manslaughter or murder linked to church activity;
- dismissal of staff, especially if it involves sexual impropriety or harassment or dishonesty;
- sexual abuse of children;
- rape – involving clergy, church members and/or church staff;
- allegations of sexual impropriety against the priest;
- allegations of financial impropriety against the priest.

We define crisis as *the moment when a series of events, apparently under control, coalesce to form a single public and uncontrollable event, with its own energy and momentum, attracting wider public and media attention.*

Some of these crises are totally outside our control and could not have been prevented by anything we might have done or any policy we might have adopted. The risk of others happening could certainly be reduced by the implementation of proper policies and by taking care. A further group are, in a way, engineered by those who want to damage the church or the priest. It is these that concern us here.

What to do in a crisis

What qualities are needed to deal with a crisis?

- Patience
- Communication
- Caution
- Resilience
- Tenacity
- Charity

First, **patience**. Few crises are improved by rapid action. Dealing with people is not like putting a fire out using an extinguisher. Those responsible for precipitating a crisis want to generate anger, discomfort and anxiety. Angry people often do the wrong thing. 'The two most powerful warriors,' Russian Commander-in-chief Prince Kutuzov told Prince Andrei before the battle of Borodino, in Tolstoy's *War and Peace*, 'are *patience and time*: they will do everything.' And again he said: 'When in doubt, my dear fellow, do nothing.' 'Do nothing' is good advice for at least early on in a crisis, when it is not clear which way things will go: anything you do then will almost certainly be wrong. There are two exceptions to this rule: they concern communication and compliance with the law.

Second, **communication**. Communicate with those who count. This is the first exception to the 'do nothing' rule. Bishops and archdeacons don't like surprises, nor do churchwardens. Tell those who need to know. If there is likely to be press coverage, talk to the diocesan communications or press officer.

Third, **caution**. Be cautious. Be careful of the content of your communications. They are not privileged and could be used in any subsequent disciplinary hearing. Remember that an 'authorized complainant' under the Ecclesiastical Jurisdiction Measure is one authorized *by the bishop*. Be careful whom you trust with important or potentially damaging information.

Fourth, **resilience**. Handling a major crisis is not unlike dealing with bereavement or serious illness. It consumes significant amounts of physical, mental and emotional energy. It will generate a whole range of emotions that you need to cope with: disappointment, anger, excitement, anxiety, hope, despair, relief. It may also give rise to physical symptoms – migraine and headaches, cramps, and digestive problems among them. If you have a physical way of manifesting stress, then it will make itself present. You will need to be resilient, to use all your coping strategies, and to call for support from your friends. Spiritual resilience is also needed and it is more important than ever to be regular in prayer. The psalmist can be a great comfort when one is under attack. The French foreign minister, diplomat and former Bishop of Autun, Prince Talleyrand, recommended the employment of 'force that resists obstacles'. He was speaking, says one biographer, not of aggressive force but of 'resistive force'. At the height of his power, his intransigence wore out opponents and he conquered them by attrition; his patience demoralized them. The obstacle faded away, leaving Talleyrand intact. This is the sort of resilience needed in a crisis (and Talleyrand faced many crises).

Fifth, **tenacity**. A crisis will pass, leaving us relieved, but certain types of event have an aftershock or a series of aftershocks, and energy must be rebuilt in order to cope with them. If there are investigations or legal proceedings, they will inevitably take time and you will need to deal with the process and the consequences. Although with the passing of the immediate crisis you may have returned to a normal pattern of work, you must also give attention to the matter that precipitated the crisis. When people decide to attack us, they are unlikely to give up if not initially successful. Handling the aftermath of a crisis is like long-term convalescence: you think you have your health back and the disease has abated, and it returns.

Sixth, **charity**. There is very little point being a priest, or even a Christian, if we handle a crisis in exactly the same way as non-Christians. Christian charity can be very very difficult when our accusers have heaped abuse on us – usually without giving us a chance to respond. Even if we cannot initially love our enemies, we can at least pray for those who persecute us. Charity must, nevertheless, be tempered by theological realism. There is a demonic dimension; it can enter the church and can be cloaked in religion. The weakness that is a source of your strength in ministry can become the focus of this demonic interest. Remember, God and the Devil are both interested in weakness. Under God, Peter's denial of Jesus became a source of strength, after the risen Lord elicited his response of love and affirmed him as a shepherd. The Devil ensured that Judas's weakness led to an act of betrayal that resulted in the passion of Christ and the death of the betrayer. Jesus' attitude to demons was simple: 'Shut up and get out.' We do not want to suggest that all or even the majority of crises are caused by demonic activity rather than human wickedness and weakness, but the demonic force itself is a force of disorder; unable to defeat or overthrow us because of Christ's victory, it attempts to divert us from our primary purposes and to drain our energy and resources.

Dealing with the press

What do you do when the *Daily Mail* and the *Sun* call you? First, don't be surprised and don't sound surprised. If you visit their websites, you will see that they invite people with stories to contact them. The quickest way to damage someone's reputation is to pass a story to the tabloid press. They will often contact the diocesan press or communications office or the bishop or archdeacon's office for comment as well. They may also turn up on your front doorstep, complete with photographer. So, don't be surprised. You may expect press interest and the only question is when it will come. The press work to very short timescales and today's interview with you will appear in tomorrow's paper.

If you sense that some parochial incident will be taken up by the press, and nearly everything from a whiff of scandal to a row over artificial flowers and grave inscriptions is of interest to them, then talk to the diocesan press officer, and agree an initial statement. It is likely to be short and to the point. There will almost certainly be a need for subsequent comment but initially you are buying time. What you want to know is the nature of the story they have. If the story was given to them deliberately by a source hostile to you, you should expect the worst. One priest accused of having an 'inappropriate relationship' with a parishioner was faced by a statement that he had announced to the congregation that he was

going to live with his 'mistress' even though he was away on holiday with his wife at the time the announcement was supposed to
have been made.

How do you deal with such a claim? If it is just totally absurd,
devoid of any shred of truth, you deny it and that denial will usually be accepted unless the journalist has clear evidence to the
contrary. You are, however, rarely presented with something as
straightforward as that. Newspapers are required to 'distinguish
clearly between comment, conjecture and fact', but a journalist on
the phone or at the front door may not do that. A story may contain some truth, some untruth, some rumour, some conjecture, and
some comment. It is not easy to distinguish the parts and the
journalist who contacts you might well be on a 'fishing expedition'
hoping to get a story. If you cannot make an outright denial, it is
better to make no comment. Unfortunately that may come out as
'Asked to deny the allegation, the Vicar said "I've no comment to
make one way or the other."' That is still better than saying something 'off the cuff' but not off the record and subsequently being
shown to have been wrong or untruthful. One should try to avoid
the actual words 'no comment' if at all possible. You might say,
depending on the circumstances 'You will understand that I cannot
comment on this matter because . . . (it is the subject of legal action,
it involves an employment issue, it involves issues of confidentiality,
etc.)'

It is quite important to understand what interests the press as
far as the church is concerned. According to a former religious cor-
respondent, the press finds us a source of news stories – news being
defined as 'a disruption of the norm' – when we show ourselves as
the **naughty church** (clergy behaving badly, fingers in the till), the
quaint church (full of curious customs), the **daft church** (think of
the Lincoln cathedral saga), the **oblivious church** (still hung up on
old issues – women, gays, pre-marital sex), the **self-important
church** (distant, defensive, devious), the **extremely established
church** (doing odd things with pageantry, the royal connection)
and the **church that really counts** (criticizing government, anti-war,
heroic work in inner cities). For journalists, the church is an
institution as untrustworthy as any other, and, unless we see the
possibility of really good publicity (and fundraising), we treat the
press with fear and suspicion.

If a member of the press rings you, follow a procedure like this, adapting it to your circumstances:

1   Find out who you are talking to and the agency, newspaper, radio or TV station involved (and details of the programme, if applicable); get the telephone number of the journalist and any other contact details. Check whether they are staff or freelance.

2   Find out the nature of the call, enquiry or allegation. You do not have to answer a question there and then. Offer to call back. Decide on a course of action. Seek advice, if necessary. Use your agreed statement.

3   Be brief, be factual, be firm, be friendly. Answer questions in a complete sentence; try to avoid 'yes' and 'no'.

4   Be prepared for cross-examination and even for argument: the reporter wants to elicit a useful comment. If you are indiscreet, your indiscretion will be reported.

5   Do not allow yourself to be bullied. You are not bound to answer every question.

Papers are ephemeral. A story may run for a day or two and then run out of steam. Your basic intention must be (a) to limit damage, and (b) to starve the story of oxygen. Those who have fed the story to the press will be trying to increase damage and to keep the story going. They will attempt to draw it to the attention of as many people as possible. They will look for other related stories that can return attention to the original story. They are aided in this by the way newspapers work. A story in a local paper may be picked up by a national newspaper and vice versa, so initial press interest generates further activity. In a similar way, a Sunday paper may follow up a story already published by its weekday counterpart. There are also freelance journalists who scan each day's papers looking for a good story to follow up. They then ring you or email you asking if you would like to comment on the original story or suggesting that they are looking at other aspects of your ministry, former parishes, etc., and offering you an opportunity to put the record straight. Whereas newsdesk journalists will normally ask for comment, those responsible for features may not do so but re-work and elaborate what has been done already. Every now and then a journalist may call to see if there have been any developments or to check a story, such as a rumour that you have resigned.

What protection and opportunity for redress do you have? Very little. The best thing to do is also the hardest: ignore it. The situation has hardly changed in nearly two hundred years. In the 1830s in France, Dorothea, Duchess of Dino, niece by marriage to Talleyrand, wrote this to a friend:

> Living as I have done in the house of Monsieur de Talleyrand and in his confidence, how could I escape the licence of the Press and its attacks in this most libellous age of journalism? It was long before I got used to it. I used to be deeply wounded, very much upset and very unhappy and I shall never become completely indifferent . . . However, as it would be equally absurd to allow one's peace of mind to be at the mercy of people one despises, I have made up my mind to read nothing of this kind, and the more directly concerned I am the less I want to know about it. I do not wish to know the evil which people think or say or write about me or about my friends.[27]

At much the same time in England Lord Melbourne complained about the press, saying that newspapers were things that 'cannot be helped . . . and therefore must be endured'. There was no remedy for the irritant and no point denying newspaper reports because 'Denials have great disadvantage – they act as compleat admissions in all cases in which you do not deny.' Finally, Lord Melbourne saw absolutely no point in initiating prosecutions:

> The real fact is that prosecutions are subject to so many objections, liable to so many difficulties, followed by so many consequences, which entirely counteract their effect, that they are no check whatever upon the violence and malignity of the press, which however, if not checked, must ultimately destroy all the institutions of the country.[28]

Alastair Campbell would almost certainly agree, especially with regard to the 'vile *Daily Mail*' (his words).

There are two codes that govern the behaviour of journalists and the press. The first is the National Union of Journalists (NUJ) Code of Conduct. It lays a duty on journalists to 'maintain the highest professional and ethical standards'. It is clear, however, that what journalists mean by 'ethical' might be thought by some, at least, of us to be 'unethical'. A journalist is to 'strive to ensure that the information he/she disseminates is fair and accurate, avoid the expression of comment and conjecture as established fact and falsification by distortion, selection or misrepresentation'. A journalist shall also 'rectify promptly any harmful inaccuracies, ensure that correction and apologies receive due prominence and afford the right of reply to a person criticised when the issue is of sufficient importance'. What appears at first sight to be a helpful principle is, almost certainly, stripped of its strength by the key words 'harmful' and 'sufficient'. Who will determine what is harmful and when something is sufficiently important, the journalist or the person or institution featured in the report or story?

There is also the Press Complaints Commission which has a Code of Practice to be found at <http://www.pcc.org.uk/cop/cop.asp>. It sets out the obligations of the press and the limitations imposed on certain types of information-gathering activity. It expresses the tensions to be found between Article 8 (right to privacy) and Article 10 (freedom of expression) in the European Convention on Human Rights. The Code is described as the 'cornerstone of self-regulation' and the preface states: 'It is essential to the workings of an agreed code that it be honoured not only to the letter but in the full spirit. The Code should not be interpreted so narrowly as to compromise its commitment to respect the rights of the individual, nor so broadly that it prevents publication in the public interest.'

Newspapers and periodicals must 'take care not to publish inaccurate, misleading or distorted materials including pictures'. The first question about a report is, therefore, 'is it accurate?' If it isn't, then you are free to write to the editor, to state the facts, and to ask for a correction. The Code provides that 'Whenever it is recognised that a significant inaccuracy, misleading statement or distorted report has been published, it must be corrected promptly and with due prominence' and also provides that an apology must be published 'whenever appropriate'. In seeking a correction – to which you feel entitled – you may, however, be drawing attention back to the original story and providing it with oxygen. Diocesan press officers tend to advise against doing anything that keeps a critical story going, but you may think it better to ask for a correction and an apology if appropriate. The Code also provides for an opportunity to reply to inaccuracies.

The Code has a section devoted to privacy which states: 'Everyone is entitled to respect for his or her private and family life, home, health and correspondence. A publication will be expected to justify intrusions into an individual's private life without consent.'

It also has sections dealing with harassment, children in general, children in sex cases, listening devices, hospitals, reporting of crime, journalistic misrepresentation or subterfuge, but these, and certain other clauses, are modified by the 'public interest' clause. Public interest includes:

1 detecting or exposing crime or a serious misdemeanour;
2 protecting public health and safety;
3 preventing the public being misled by some statement or action of an individual or organization.

As the clergy are public figures whose behaviour is governed by ecclesiastical law and by a code of conduct, the press can reasonably claim a 'public interest' for many stories about the clergy and their alleged failings. If a cleric claims violation of privacy, harassment or misrepresentation, then the publication is likely to claim 'public interest' in the church and the clergy. If a complaint is made to the Press Complaints Commission, however, and it appears that the Code has been breached, the newspaper will have to give a full explanation 'demonstrating how the public interest was served'.

Making a complaint to the Press Complaints Commission is very easy. You should first of all write to the editor of the newspaper to seek the correction of an inaccuracy or an apology for an intrusion. If the editor does not reply, or you are unhappy with the reply, then write to the Press Complaints Commission at 1 Salisbury Square, London EC4Y 8JB. First check the Code of Practice and determine which article you think has been breached. Then summarize your complaint in a letter, give the name of the publication and the date on which it was published, identify the appropriate section of the Code and explain why you think it has been breached. Send a copy of the offending article, making sure that the name of the publication is clear, together with copies of any other relevant correspondence.

The complaint should be made within one month of the publication of the article or, if you have taken the matter up with the editor, up to one month after the end of a continuous correspondence. It is also possible to lodge your complaint via the Press Complaints Commission website <http://www.pcc.org.uk/complaint/how_complaint.htm>.

The Commission may decide that your complaint is not one they can deal with or determine that there has been no breach of the Code. If they think that there has been a breach, then a copy of the complaint is sent to the editor and your comments are invited on any response. Further information and comments may be required as an investigation continues. The Commission will work for a solution acceptable to both sides, but if such a resolution is not possible then it may adjudicate on the complaint and, if it is upheld, require the publication to publish it with due prominence.

In pursuing what the NUJ Code calls 'overriding considerations of public interest', a journalist might obtain information or photographs by other than straightforward means. The Press Complaints Commission's Code requires journalists not to engage in 'intimidation, harassment or persistent pursuit' and says that they must not 'persist in questioning, telephoning, pursuing or photographing individuals once asked to desist'. Again, however, the journalist or his or her editor may claim 'public interest'. Protection against press harassment is provided by the Harassment Act 1997 and a priest who feels that he or she is being harassed should not hesitate to inform the police. The Act states (s. 1) that:

A person must not pursue a course of conduct
a) which amounts to harassment of another, and
b) which he knows or ought to know amounts to harassment of the other.

Section 7 of the Act defines 'harassment' as including causing alarm or causing distress and states that a 'course of conduct' – to be harassment – must involve conduct on at least two occasions. In certain rather rare circumstances the publication of articles by a newspaper could amount to harassment, as was held in the case of Esther Thomas v. News Group Newspapers (The *Sun*) [2001]. In that judgment, Lord Phillips, the Master of the Rolls, said:

[32] Whether conduct is reasonable will depend upon the circumstances of the particular case. When considering whether the conduct of the press in publishing articles is reasonable for the purposes of the 1997 Act, the answer does not turn upon whether opinions expressed in the article are reasonably held. The question must be answered by reference to the right of the press to freedom of expression which has been so emphatically recognized by the jurisprudence both of Strasbourg and this country.

[33] Prior to the 1997 Act, the freedom with which the press could publish facts or opinions about individuals was circumscribed by the law of defamation. Protection of reputation is a legitimate reason to restrict freedom of expression. Subject to the law of defamation, the press was entitled to publish an article, or series of articles, about an individual, notwithstanding that it could be foreseen that such conduct was likely to cause distress to the subject of the article.

[34] The 1997 Act has not rendered such conduct unlawful. In general, press criticism, even if robust, does not constitute unreasonable conduct and does not fall within the natural meaning of harassment. A pleading, which does no more than allege that the defendant newspaper has published a series of articles that have foreseeably caused distress to an individual, will be susceptible to a strike-out on the ground that it discloses no arguable case of harassment.

Recourse to law, whether for defamation or a civil action for harassment, is unlikely to be an option that can be pursued by the clergy. The financial costs are simply too great. The law of defamation covers libel (defamation in a permanent form, including email libel) and slander. Anyone may be sued for either originating or disseminating defamatory material. Essentially, the only defence is to demonstrate to the satisfaction of a jury that the supposedly defamatory claim is true. There is also the defence of 'fair comment', where the defendant has to satisfy the jury that the opinion was honestly held and not that it was factually true. The costs of defamation cases can be extremely high but if successful the damages awarded by the jury can be crippling.

Journalists will not reveal their sources; indeed the Code states that journalists have a 'moral obligation to protect confidential sources of information' and the cleric subjected to 'exposure' in a newspaper may well be disturbed by this. It can further undermine confidence as you wonder who might have said what and in what context. An article that draws on many such sources will identify them by labels such as 'in the words of one parishioner' and 'regulars at the church say', as well as 'parish gossip', 'local rumour' and the like. One rarely has to look further than those with whom one has already had difficulties and those who regularly copy their letters to bishop and archdeacon. A priest may also find that he or she is bound by a similar moral obligation and is unable to use knowledge, obtained in confidential settings – pastoral conversation, counselling and confession – in defence of his or her own position. Accused, for example, by a third party, of bringing about the break-up of a marriage, the priest, who may well know many of the details of a series of complex relationships between parishioners, nevertheless cannot disclose this material and is rendered silent and, apparently, defenceless. But, of course, one is not and, other than the correction of straightforward and potentially damaging matters of fact, the best advice remains that of Lord Melbourne: it cannot be helped, so it must be endured.

Ministering out of weakness

Although theoretically and theologically the church authorities acknowledge that all the clergy are earthenware vessels, fallible human beings beset by 'unruly wills and affections', this theoretical and theological knowledge may not carry over into practice, not least because bishops and archdeacons are themselves accountable, fear scandal, and do not necessarily think coolly and clearly in a crisis. You may have done something foolish or something wrong. You have erred. You have left undone what you ought to have done. You have done what you ought not to have done. You have erred through ignorance, through weakness, and, occasionally perhaps, through your own deliberate fault. Examining your conscience, you are alert to your failing, whether it be one-off or habitual. You have done what you can to remedy your fault, including confession to a priest, if this is part of your tradition, and the seeking of advice. You have resolved 'not to sin again'. You may, however, find yourself in one of two or three positions: you feel you must talk to your bishop about the matter, or the person against whom you have erred tells you of their intention to make it known, or somehow it has become, if not common knowledge, then at least known to one or two people, and you fear a scandal of some sort.

Speaking to your bishop as your 'father in God' may seem, quite rightly, to be a reasonable thing to do. In virtue of his office, he has a duty of care towards you. If you have lost your faith, if you find yourself completely at odds with the Church of England, if your spouse has deserted you, if you find ministry an unbearable burden, if you are burnt out and unable to cope any longer, go and see your bishop. He will respond pastorally. He will ensure that the resources available for care and counselling are brought to bear. He will aid you in reaching necessary decisions.

If you have become emotionally or sexually involved with a parishioner, if you have been 'salami slicing' the Sunday collection, if you are dependent on alcohol or addicted to drugs, if you have committed a crime, do not turn *first of all* to your bishop because *he will need to respond to what you tell him in his disciplinary and judicial role rather than his pastoral role.* He will be caught in precisely the dual-role relationship dilemma that we identified earlier. Speak first, and urgently, to a lawyer or, if you are a member, to an Amicus adviser, or to someone who can offer you objective advice. Decide with your lawyer or other adviser on an appropriate response to events. Then ask to see the bishop, indicating in general terms the sort of matter you wish to see him about, and go accompanied by your lawyer or adviser. Remember that, quite apart from a proper desire to put your own house in order and to be reconciled to God and neighbour, you are dealing with the practical realities of job, income and housing. These are not considerations that can be ignored at this stage. Resist the confessional urge, the desire to tell the bishop everything, no matter how strong it may be. There is a proper disciplinary procedure that will take its course and that procedure is designed to respect your human rights as well as the rights of anyone against whom you may have sinned. Do not abandon your rights at this stage, no matter how guilty and contrite you may feel. What you most need at this point is external, objective advice. Do not see the bishop, archdeacon, rural dean, or anyone sent by them or on their behalf, alone.

Do not resign. Do not offer to resign. Do not accept encouragement to resign. The new Clergy Discipline Measure wisely guards against resignation as an immediate response to an allegation. If you have broken the rules, be prepared to deal with the consequences in a mature, responsible, adult and Christian way. If the bishop, through an appointed complainant, brings a formal complaint against you, then you will be asked whether you admit or deny the complaint. You must answer truthfully. If you admit the complaint, then the disciplinary consequences can be determined by the bishop. Your representative can present mitigating factors (sorrow for what has happened, uncharacteristic moment of weakness, effect of stress, undertaking counselling, dealing with drug or alcohol dependency, etc.) which must be taken into consideration. If you deny the complaint made against you, because it is untrue or because the complaint as put does not describe what you have done, then the matter is decided by a tribunal in the process already described.

The crucial question has nothing at all to do with disciplinary proceedings and codes of conduct. It is the question put to Simon, son of John, by Jesus after his passion, death, and resurrection, that is to say, after Peter's denial of his Lord: 'Do you love me?' If you can answer, truthfully and from the heart, 'Yes, Lord, you know everything, you know that I love you', then weakness can be turned to strength. You may have to minister at another place, in another time; you may have to accept humbly discipline imposed upon you, but you did not choose him, he chose you, and you are a priest for ever 'after the order of Melchisedech'. But if you cannot say 'Yes, Lord', then you should no longer presume to feed the flock of Christ or to tend his sheep. If you cannot make an answer, if it is 'I don't know, Lord', then you need time to recover your spiritual sense and to find an answer to the question. If the answer is 'No', then the course of action is obvious, though it might still be as well to take further counsel before making that decision.

Conclusion:
A ministry worth all its pains

Parish ministry as we see it today has changed dramatically. It has done so in a very short period of time. The change has been generated both within the structures of the church – by the ordination of women, by changed priorities in ministry, by the response to reduced resources and the need to provide for pensions – and by forces outside the church – social, political and economic conditions, extension of regulation, response to abuse. To be effective, a priest must be adaptable. The ministry to which a priest is called, the ministry received as a gift, is none other than the ministry of Christ himself, and when we think of survival in ministry, of being oppressed by the burden, of coping with crises, of being criticized and misunderstood, then we must think of Christ in his passion, and of Paul being poured out as an oblation. The Prayer Book Palm Sunday collect offers the example of Jesus' great humility, and makes the prayer that should be ours in adversity 'that we may both follow the example of his patience, and also be made partakers of his resurrection'.

To illustrate this, let us turn to Maundy Thursday, to the solemn remembrance of our Lord's last supper with his disciples, his prediction of the immediacy of his betrayal, his washing of the disciples' feet, his institution of the Holy Eucharist, his agony in the garden, and his arrest, and think of his instructions to his disciples prior to the supper. As Passover approached he sent Peter and John into the city, charging them to prepare everything so that they might eat Passover together. They were told how to find the house and the householder. We do not know who he was or how he was known to Jesus, but they were to ask him, in their Master's name, 'Where is the guest room, where I am to eat the Passover with my disciples?' And he would show them a large upper room furnished; there they were to make ready.

Where is the guest room? asks Jesus. Where is the room where I am welcome, the room furnished ready to receive me? We may notice three things here: it is a guest room, a room for others rather than for the householder; it is a place in which the guest is made welcome; and it is furnished with what is necessary. The disciples will need to complete the preparations but it is already furnished with whatever is necessary. We may recall what Jesus told the disciples when he sent them out ahead of him: how they were to stay wherever they were made welcome, and how their blessing was to rest upon the house and its occupants.

We have here, of course, a spiritual analogy. It is not hard for us to make the connections. The language of evangelical conversion includes many metaphors that involve accepting the Lord as saviour, opening the heart to him, welcoming him in. We are to be that chamber, that guest room, ready to receive so precious a guest. It is, if you like, a part of us, an essential part of us, that is not ours because it is willingly surrendered to the one who would occupy it. Yet so essential is it, that the occupant of the room changes the nature of the entire dwelling, such that nothing remains the same.

Jesus uses this sort of language when talking of demonic possession – being possessed, controlled by, owned by, demonic forces, also called in Scripture unclean spirits. He speaks of the possessed person being exorcized and preparing that inner chamber for another guest, and finding that it is impossible to resist the other demons, more wicked still, brought there by the one who had formerly claimed possession and been expelled. We may not be very comfortable speaking of devils and demons. We do not really see the world in that way any more and we may be rightly suspicious of churches that see every setback in terms of demonic attack. But there is a demonic dimension and on the Maundy Thursday night, of course, we see the figure of Simon Iscariot's son, Judas, slipping away into the darkness and Luke is not afraid to say of him that Satan had entered him. We cannot entirely renounce the world view, the cosmic view, of the New Testament, which includes the attack of and heavenly warfare with demonic forces. We are aware of these forces, whatever post-Enlightenment name we give them. They are the forces of disorder.

A demon is a malignant being of superhuman nature. That is the definition in the *Shorter Oxford Dictionary*. The word 'malignant' is well chosen, for as early as 1591 it meant one keenly desirous of the misfortune of another or, indeed, of others generally. We are not susceptible to takeover, to demonic possession but we are open to it if we neglect or compromise our spiritual immune system, and it is possible to invite into one's inner chamber that malign power, just as it is possible to invite Christ in. And the possessed do not suddenly rant and rave and utter blasphemies; no, they are capable of wrapping themselves in a cloak of religion, just as Mephistopheles appeared to Doctor Faustus in the habit of a friar. This malignant power then focuses on weakness of any sort.

This is a matter vital to ministry. The minister of the Gospel is called by God and his or her vocation is confirmed by the church. God is sovereign; he calls whom he will, and he is much less interested in selection criteria than the church is. We see the call coming to those who are marked by a wound that penetrates their entire being – it comes to Jacob, to Joseph, to Moses, to Samson, to David and to Solomon, to Elijah, Amos and Jeremiah, to Jonah and to Job, as also to Peter and to Paul. Their strength is born out of their weakness. God takes a weakness and makes it a strength. But the demonic force is interested only in making a weakness a portal to shame and disgrace, while claiming, constantly claiming, that all this is for the good. Jesus came to heal the sick; the Devil wants them shamed, shunned, cast out. God and the Devil are interested, therefore, in the same thing. In God's hands, Peter's weakness is turned, through the dreadful experience of denial, into strength. In the Devil's hands, Judas's weakness becomes the means by which Jesus is betrayed and Judas himself destroyed. And if we are inclined to think this an exceptional dichotomy, then we must think of the other disciples. The Evangelist reports that they all asked 'Is it me, Lord?' Now why would you ask this question if you had within you no possibility of betraying Jesus? They were uncertain. They had to ask for confirmation.

Where is the guest room ready furnished where I will eat with my disciples? Can we say, 'Here it is, Lord'? The question is put to us most acutely as we focus on Maundy Thursday. It is the night of the Lord's betrayal. It is the night when he knows who his friends are. Will we be counted among them? There are alternatives.

Accepting the demonic can be a path to easy glory, to wealth even, and to fame, though the fame may turn to infamy. Repayments are initially easy but in the end the person who willingly accepts the entrance of the malign force becomes not the willing agent but the possession of that force. It is the ultimate betrayal. It is worse than disbelief. It mocks Christ. Woe to that man by whom the Son of God is betrayed.

But there are other alternatives. Closing up the guest room and closing in on oneself, being unwilling to make any commitment, becoming self-obsessed. Letting it out without enthusiasm, to this guest and that, unwilling to decide, unwilling to commit, sampling the spiritual buffet but never resolving the question. There is taking in a guest, like a landlady of old, on her terms, not theirs, unwilling to change to accommodate this or any guest. And there is the choice that we made at baptism, at confirmation, at ordination, when we accepted the gift of ministry – making Christ fully welcome, making the guest room over to him, accepting his promise to come and dwell and to eat and drink with you.

The Gospels present us with a picture of Christ's abundant love – 'generous love' Newman calls it – the love that reaches out to us, that holds us, that grasps us and will not let us go until we know ourselves as loved and know who it is that loves us; the love that weeps for us, suffers for us, bleeds for us, dies for us; the love that tends our wounds, and hides our weaknesses, and wraps us in the mantle of mercy and forgiveness. This is the love of him who says 'This is my body broken for you', 'This is my blood shed for you' – for *you* the one whom I *love*. How can we contemplate this love and not weep, weep for joy, weep with relief, weep in amazement that anyone can love us so, let alone the one in whom is found all that is good and beautiful, weep that he should have chosen us to share this ministry of love. Jesus, as we have already noted, will say to Peter, after his death, after his passing through death: 'Simon, son of John, do you love me?' And Peter will choke, and be his wonderfully impatient self, and be vexed at being asked three times, but he will say it: 'You know everything, Lord; you know that I love you.' Judas cannot say it. The slanderer, the betrayer, the malignant shows that he is entirely without love. He wants only harm; he is keenly desirous of the misfortune of another. And the sign of affection, the loving kiss, becomes a mockery. But Peter for all his many faults can say it and he means it: You know that I love you. As long as we can say it, ministry is worth all its pains.

Resources for survival in the parish

Other books and publications

Craig, Yvonne J., *Peacemaking for Churches*, London, SPCK, 1999.

Dudley, Martin R., *A Manual for Ministry to the Sick*, London, SPCK, 1997.

Dudley, Martin R. and Rounding, Virginia, *Churchwardens: A Survival Guide*, London, SPCK, 2003.

Forster, Mark, *Get Everything Done and Still Have Time to Play*, London, Hodder & Stoughton, 2000.

Forster, Mark, *How to Make Your Dreams Come True*, London, Hodder & Stoughton, 2002.

Hanchey, Howard, *Church Growth and the Power of Evangelism*, Cambridge, Mass., Cowley, 1990.

Hulme, William E., *Managing Stress in Ministry*, San Francisco, Harper & Row, 1985.

Lebacqz, Karen and Barton, Ronald G., *Sex in the Parish*, Louisville, Ky., Westminster/John Knox Press, 1991.

Lee, Carl and Horsman, Sarah, *Affirmation and Accountability*, Dunsford, The Society of Mary and Martha, 2002.

Nelson, John (ed.), *Leading, Managing, Ministering*, Norwich, Canterbury Press, 1999.

Nelson, John (ed.), *Management and Ministry*, Norwich, Canterbury Press, 1996.

Nouwen, Henri, *The Wounded Healer*, New York, Doubleday, 1972.

Oswald, Roy M., *Clergy Self-Care: Finding A Balance for Effective Ministry*, New York, Alban Institute, 1991.

Oswald, Roy M. and Kroeger, Otto, *Personality Type and Religious Leadership*, New York, Alban Institute, 1991.

Rediger, G. Lloyd, *Ministry and Sexuality*, Minneapolis, Fortress Press, 1990.

Sanford, John A., *Ministry Burnout*, New York, Paulist Press, 1982.

Sedgwick, Timothy F., *The Making of Ministry*, Boston, Mass., Cowley, 1993.

Snow, John, *The Impossible Vocation: Ministry in the Mean Time*, Cambridge, Mass., Cowley, 1988.

Warren, Yvonne, *The Cracked Pot*, Stowmarket, Kevin Mayhew, 2002.
Wiest, Walter E. and Smith, E. A., *Ethics in Ministry: A Guide for the Professional*, Minneapolis, Fortress Press, 1990.

Organizations and services

Administry

A missionary organization dedicated to helping churches grow, Administry believes in good administration as a part of ministry, and that good organization and administration is about:

- order and peace, not chaos and hurt
- clarity and simplicity, not confusion and bureaucracy
- people and their value, not paper and systems.

They provide training and resources in the coordination and organization of most aspects of church life for leaders, administrators and church members.

Address: Administry
                   62 Farm Road
                   Rowley Regis
                   Birmingham B65 8ET
Tel.:   0845 128 5177
Fax: 0845 128 5188
Email: mail@administry.co.uk
Website: http://www.administry.co.uk

Amicus

The trade union for the voluntary sector, including a section for clergy and other church workers. The advantages of membership include free representation in the event of a problem of any kind. (An Amicus spokesman reports: 'We frequently have clergy who have difficulties with higher clergy – e.g. archdeacon, bishop etc., parishioners and others – and we represent them informally or formally. Sometimes this includes giving legal advice all of which is free to Amicus members.') Amicus has taken cases as far as the Privy Council on behalf of clergy members, and will represent them in the tribunals to be set up under the Clergy Discipline Measure and the Employment Tribunals when the church grants access to them under the proposed legislation. Amicus can also deal with claims concerning accidents and personal injuries etc., they offer free professional indemnity insurance for all their clergy members and also offer excellent learning opportunities. You need to have been a member for six months before being eligible to receive these benefits; someone contacting Amicus with a problem who is not yet a member but is willing to become one may receive advice though not direct help. Membership contributions are currently just under £10 a month (less for concessions).

Address:	Janet Golds
	Amicus
	Non Profit Sector National Office
	40 Bermondsey Street
	London SE1 3UD
Tel.:	020 7939 7008
Fax:	020 7357 6425
Email:	Janet.Golds@amicus-m.org
Website:	http://www.3rdsectorunion.org.uk/clergy.shtml

Bridge Builders

A programme run by the London Mennonite Trust (registered charity no. 227410), Bridge Builders provides training, mediation, consultancy and related services for all Christian churches and denominations in Britain. The programme's vision grows out of the historical Mennonite commitment to the way of peace and non-retaliation against enemies. Bridge Builders offers training workshops and courses in handling and transforming conflict within the church, as well as mediation and intervention services to individuals, church leadership teams and congregations. Consultancy services on offer range from brief telephone conversations to intensive coaching on planning strategies and managing oneself in situations of conflict.

Address:	Alastair McKay
	Director of Bridge Builders
	London Mennonite Centre
	14 Shepherds Hill
	London N6 5AQ
Tel.:	0845 4500 214
Fax:	020 8341 6807
Email:	AlastairMcKay@menno.org.uk
Website:	http://www.menno.org.uk

Centre for Christian Communication

A research, resource and teaching centre established in 1996 for lay and ordained Christians, located in the north east of England. Through conferences and training workshops, the Centre aims to provide stimulating practical help with modern methods of communication. The principal areas covered are: preaching in contemporary culture, apologetics in post-modern societies, and communication skills and media awareness for church leaders.

Address: Centre for Christian Communication
          Cross Gate Centre
          Alexandra Crescent
          Durham DH1 4HF
Tel.:   0191 374 4405
Fax: 0191 374 4401
Website: http://www.xiancomm.org.uk/

College of Counsellors

A confidential counselling service for church members, church leaders and clergy of the Diocese of Durham which involves working with a professionally trained counsellor over a number of sessions, in complete privacy. The service is confidential. In exceptional cases (such as where a child or a life may be at risk), confidentiality would be reviewed with the counsellor.

Address: Mrs Alison Moore
          Bishop's Adviser in Pastoral Care and Counselling
          1 West View
          New Brancepeth
          Durham DH7 7ET
Email: Alison.Moore@durham.anglican.org
Website: http://www.durham.anglican.org/information/collegeofcounsel-
          lors.htm

Communications Training

A programme offered by the Church of England to help individuals and organizations get to grips with questions such as:

- What is your message?
- Who are you trying to reach?
- Where does your audience get its information?
- When are they most receptive?
- Why should they listen to you?

The programme includes courses in crisis management and how to deal with the media during a crisis.

Address: Communications Training
           Church House
           Great Smith Street
           London SW1P 3NZ
Tel.:   020 7898 1458 or 020 7898 1465
Fax: 020 7222 6672
Email: comms.training@c-of-e.org.uk
Website: http://www.commstraining.cofe.anglican.org

The English Clergy Association

Founded in 1938, the Association lists as its aims: 'to support all Clerks in Holy Orders in their vocation and ministry; to oppose unnecessary bureaucracy in the Church; to monitor legislative and other processes of change; and to promote in every available way the good of English Parish and Cathedral life and the welfare of clergy.' It also provides modest grants for holidays.

Address: The Revd John Masding
           The Old School
           Norton Hawkfield
           Pensford
           Bristol BS39 4HB
Email: masding@breathe.co.uk
Website: http://www.clergyassoc.co.uk/content/home.htm

The Grubb Institute

The Grubb Institute was set up in 1969 to contribute to 'the well being and wholeness of society by enabling persons, communities and institutions to transform to meet real human need'. Using expertise developed from the human sciences and applied Christian theology, the Institute provides consultancy and action research to education, health, social care, religious and voluntary organizations and businesses.

Address: The Grubb Institute
           Cloudesley Street
           London N1 0HU
Tel./Fax: 020 7278 8061
Email: info@grubb.org.uk
Website: http://www.grubb.org.uk

IDCS

The Inter-Diocesan Counselling Service for the Dioceses of Blackburn,
Carlisle, Chester, Liverpool and Manchester which was set up in 1984 at
the request of the north-western bishops to provide professional and
confidential counselling for individuals and couples. The Service is independent of diocesan structures but enjoys their support. Counselling is
available to all Anglican clergy of the dioceses involved, to clergy spouses
and children and to those training for ordination. Counselling is offered
for anything which causes concern or distress, as well as in the following
specific areas:

- Relationship difficulties – with spouses, other family members,
  colleagues or parishioners
- Stress within families
- Marriage breakdown
- Work-related stresses
- Individual development
- Loss and bereavement
- Addiction
- Sexual orientation
- Psychosexual problems
- Childhood abuse
- Reaction to trauma

IDCS counsellors belong to the British Association for Counselling and
abide by its code of practice. Meetings are completely confidential except
in very exceptional circumstances such as where there is a clear risk of
serious harm to the client or others.

See http://www.blackburn.anglican.org/index.htm

John Truscott

John describes his work as 'to advise and train churches, ministers and
mission agents in creative organization and people skills'. He offers
consultancy and training in the following six areas:

- Personal support for Christian leaders
- Management training for ministers and mission executives
- Structural review for trustees and church councils
- Creative tools for strategic planners
- Practical advice for Christian communicators
- Fresh thinking for administrators and helpers

Address: John Truscott
           69 Sandridge Road
           St Albans AL1 4AG
Tel./fax: 01727 832176
Email: get-help@john-truscott.co.uk
Website: http://www.john-truscott.co.uk

Modem

Modem, a national and ecumenical network (registered charity no. 1048772), exists to integrate the theory and practice of management with the theology and practice of ministry. Its vision is that, through dialogue, ministers will draw upon insights from management and managers will draw upon insights from theology and spirituality. It produces a number of interesting publications and newsletters.

Address: Peter J. Bates
           Modem Treasurer and Membership Secretary
           Carselands
           Woodmancote
           Henfield
           West Sussex BN5 9SS
Tel./fax: 01273 493172
Email: peter@bateshouse.freeserve.co.uk
Website: http://users.powernet.co.uk/harpham/index.html

The Society of Mary and Martha

Established with a particular concern to offer support to people in Christian ministry of any denomination and/or their spouses, the Society offers a programme of retreats and workshops for personal growth and spiritual development. There is also specialist support at times of stress or crisis. The Society is a registered charity (no. 327394).

Address: The Society of Mary and Martha
           The Sheldon Centre
           Dunsford
           Exeter EX6 7LE
Tel./fax: 01647 252752
Email: smm@sheldon.uk.com
Website: http://www.sheldon.uk.com/frameset.htm

Other websites

http://www.ncvo-vol.org.uk/asp/search/ncvo/main.aspx
The online 'best practice resource' of the NCVO for all matters on employment and working with volunteers.

http://www.professionals4free.org
A website which 'signposts' users to brokers of free professional services via a searchable database, designed for voluntary and community organizations and charities seeking free professional advice.

http://www.bcconnections.org.uk
The website of a charity dedicated to helping other charities obtain more support from business.

http://www.ekklesia.co.uk/
The site of Ekklesia, a think-tank that works to promote theological ideas in what it calls the 'public square'.

http://www.humansyn.co.uk/products/lsi_conflict.html
A good site from Human Synergistics on dealing with conflict.

http://www.maxamind.co.uk/index/teambuilding
A site about teambuilding using Myers Briggs and Belben methodologies.

http://www.blackburn.anglican.org/yellow_pages/index.htm
A directory of church-related services and businesses, available on the Diocese of Blackburn's site.

http://www.markforster.net/
Mark Forster's site on aspects of time and life management.

Notes

1 Yvonne Warren, *The Cracked Pot*, Stowmarket, Kevin Mayhew, 2002.
2 H. Newton Maloney and Richard A. Hunt, *The Psychology of Clergy*, Harrisburg, Penn., 1991.
3 Mark Forster, *Get Everything Done and Still Have Time to Play*, London, Hodder & Stoughton, 2000.
4 Mark Forster, *How to Make Your Dreams Come True*, London, Help Yourself, 2002.
5 Martin Dudley and Virginia Rounding, *Churchwardens: A Survival Guide*, London, SPCK, 2003.
6 Timothy F. Sedgwick, *The Making of Ministry*, Boston, Mass., Cowley, 1993.
7 Sedgwick, *The Making of Ministry*, pp. 89–90.
8 Warren, *The Cracked Pot*, p. 204.
9 Carl Lee and Sarah Horsman, *Affirmation and Accountability*, Dunsford, The Society of Mary and Martha, 2002, p. 74.
10 Warren, *The Cracked Pot*.
11 W. S. Wigglesworth, 'The Office of Churchwarden', in A. E. J. Rawlinson, *The World's Question and the Christian Answer*, London, Longman, 1944, p. 104.
12 Dudley and Rounding, *Churchwardens*, pp. 56–7.
13 Dudley and Rounding, *Churchwardens*, p. 57.
14 Dudley and Rounding, *Churchwardens*, p. 58.
15 *Ecclesiastical Law Journal*, vol. 7, no. 32, January 2003, pp. 17–30.
16 Dudley and Rounding, *Churchwardens*, pp. 77–9.
17 Dudley and Rounding, *Churchwardens*, pp. 80–1.
18 Dudley and Rounding, *Churchwardens*, pp. 82–3.
19 Dudley and Rounding, *Churchwardens*, p. 84.
20 Dudley and Rounding, *Churchwardens*, pp. 83–6.
21 From the Indiana University Health Center website.
22 From the Health and Safety Executive website.
23 Lee and Horsman, *Affirmation and Accountability*, p. 70.
24 Dudley and Rounding, *Churchwardens*, p. 84.
25 Dudley and Rounding, *Churchwardens*, pp. 87–9.

26 Privy Council Office, <http://www.privy-council.org.uk/output/
page170.asp>, Case No. 12 Cheesman v. Church Commissioners.
27 Philip Ziegler, *The Duchess of Dino*, London, Collins, 1962, pp. 152–3.
28 Quoted in L. G. Mitchell, *Lord Melbourne 1779–1848*, Oxford, OUP,
1997, p. 25.

Index